Understanding the Human Factor: Life and Its Impact
Part I

Professor Gary A. Sojka

THE TEACHING COMPANY ®

PUBLISHED BY:

THE TEACHING COMPANY
4840 Westfields Boulevard, Suite 500
Chantilly, Virginia 20151-2299
1-800-TEACH-12
Fax—703-378-3819
www.teach12.com

ISBN 1-59803-620-3

Gary A. Sojka, Ph.D.

President Emeritus and Professor Emeritus
Bucknell University

Professor Gary A. Sojka received his liberal arts education at Coe College, where he earned a B.A. in Biology with a minor in English. He holds M.S. and Ph.D. degrees in Biochemical Genetics from Purdue University. Following his graduate work, he accepted a postdoctoral appointment at Indiana University Bloomington and progressed from Research Associate in Microbiology to Full Professor and chair of the Biology Department. From that position, he was named Dean of the College of Arts and Sciences at IU Bloomington.

In 1984, Professor Sojka assumed the presidency of Bucknell University, a position he held for 11 years. During his presidency, Professor Sojka regularly taught a course in microbiology and offered guest lectures in microbiology, cell biology, and the general studies curriculum. After stepping down from the presidency, Professor Sojka taught for 11 more years (biologists love symmetry) in the Biology Department at Bucknell, where he taught the general biology course for nonmajors, the introductory biology course for majors, and microbiology and offered seminars on the domestication of plants and animals and the security of the world's food supply.

Before Professor Sojka left the presidency at Bucknell, he and his wife, Sandra, began breeding and raising endangered livestock. Professor Sojka has served as the President of the American Livestock Breeds Conservancy and The Philadelphia Society for Promoting Agriculture. He remains active in agriculture, with special interests in public policy relating to animal welfare, breed conservation, farm safety, and equine athlete health and safety. He is the recipient of IU Bloomington's Senior Class Award for Teaching Excellence and Dedication to Undergraduates, the Indiana University System Frederic Bachman Lieber Memorial Award for Distinguished Teaching, and the Sheepskin Award from the Pennsylvania Association of Colleges and Universities. He holds an honorary Doctor of Laws degree from Lycoming College and an honorary Doctor of Science degree from Purdue University.

Table of Contents
Understanding the Human Factor: Life and Its Impact
Part I

Understanding the Human Factor: Life and Its Impact

Scope:

This course deals with what some have called the most momentous inflection point in the history of our species. Though modern humans have been present on Earth for nearly 200,000 years, they spent the vast majority of that time as hunter-gatherers. It was only about 10,000 years ago that people began to exert greater control over nature and to depend more on food production than on food procurement. This change depended upon the ability of people to domesticate both plants and animals. We discuss the methods used to study this period of prehistory; trace the emergence of agriculture and permanent settlements in a number of localities on several continents and land masses; and follow their dispersal and spread. Models will be presented for how these early settled agricultural communities evolved into villages, some of which became cities or city-states. Much of what we think of as civilization arose in those early cities, none of which could have developed without plant and animal domestication to provide surplus food, hides, fibers, dung, muscle power, and mobility. We will explore the idea that the character of a culture may be due in great part to the array of potential domesticates available to it.

The second section of the course deals with the specifics of a number of early plant and animal domestications. We look first at cereal grains, which have been a major source of calories in the diets of the majority of the world's population for the last 10 millennia. The provenance of many of the common garden vegetables will be explored, as will the importance of plants that resist spoilage and can be kept during the fallow season. We will then look at the domestication of a number of animals, including dogs, cats, sheep, goats, swine, horses, asses, and chickens. The concept of what constitutes an animal breed and how it is maintained will be discussed. We also look at products derived from the milk of domesticates, such as cheese and yogurt. A brief discussion of the over 400 distinct types of cheese will be presented with an eye toward linking some of those types to specific localities or cultures. Many plants and animals have traveled far from their initial points of domestication. The Columbian exchange resulted in tomatoes, potatoes, maize, tobacco, and chocolate moving from the New World to the Old World. At the same time, wheat, oats, sugar cane, horses, and cattle crossed in the other direction. We discuss the social significance of coffee, tea, chocolate, and tobacco. A brief account of the domestication and cultivation of trees—which provide wood for pulp, construction, and fuel as well as providing a number of fruits and nuts—is followed by a discussion of some minor domesticates, including rodents, molds, bacteria, and marine creatures.

The final section of the course deals with economic, political, and scientific milestones from the 18th century to the present that had significant impacts on our relationship with our domesticates. We talk about the importance of agriculture to George Washington, Thomas Jefferson, and King George III. Their differing views of agricultural practice had a major impact on the early development of the United States. We examine the correspondence between Charles Darwin and his cousin, Francis Galton, concerning the domestication of animals, and we consider the impact of Gregor Mendel's investigations into heredity on scientific plant and animal breeding. We look at the work of several individuals on plant breeding and the development of new species, varieties, and cultivars. We then turn our attention to advances in food preservation and transportation and relate those practices to the development of a truly global food-production system. The green revolution and a system of international plant-breeding efforts have greatly increased the yields of a number of important food crops, but 50 years after this major advancement in agricultural productivity, questions are still being raised about the long-term wisdom of such approaches. Advances in molecular biology and biotechnology along with mammalian cloning techniques have added a new and exciting dimension to plant and animal breeding and management. We discuss some of the new frontiers being contemplated, including direct production of pharmaceuticals in fruit and milk and xenotransplantation of animal organs into humans. The course concludes with a discussion of modern agricultural practices and their sustainability. This is an area of intense debate around the world, and all of the preceding lectures should provide useful and broad context for addressing this subject.

We are the beneficiaries of a civilization that has come down to us as the result of 10,000 years of progress and change. We are presently facing crisis after crisis as a result of population growth, habitat destruction, water and air pollution, resource depletion, and climate change. It is hoped that this course will provide not only some useful background on how we came to be in our present state but also some hope for ways in which we can progress wisely and continue for another 10,000 years.

Lecture One
Man the Domesticator

Scope:

This course deals with the profound effect of humans' domestication of plants, animals, and microbes. The case will be made that domestication benefits both the domesticator and the domesticate. This is a multidisciplinary course, involving subjects from archaeology to molecular biology. I will also explain how I am melding my scientific background with my efforts as a plant and animal farmer focused on conservation of endangered breeds and varieties.

Outline

I. In this course we explore the role the domestication of other creatures played in the greatest transition our species has ever undergone: the change from being food procurers to being food producers.

II. This course is multidisciplinary, delving into subjects and approaches associated with anthropology, archaeology, history, sociology, geography, ecology, evolution, botany, microbiology, genetics, agronomy, molecular biology, and philosophy.

III. The course is structured in the following way.

    A. In the first few lectures, we discuss the theories that archaeologists, anthropologists, and others have constructed about the first plant and animal domestications and the transition of our species from a hunting-gathering animal to a food producer.

    B. In the next section of the course, we explore the history of the domestication of some key plants and animals.

    C. From there, we discuss the way human activities have moved plants, animals, and microbes to new habitats where some have done remarkably well.

    D. Using a few key individuals as examples, we then talk about how agricultural practice grew in importance, how it helped foster population growth and determine the fate of nations, and how it became more systematic and scientific.

E. The course also includes a discussion of exciting ways that cutting-edge techniques and approaches are building on centuries of progress in refining the management of domesticates to improve the quality and extend the length of human life.

IV. Although the course follows a rough chronological structure, we will not attempt to catalog all the achievements that occurred between the first domestication events and our efforts at engineering solutions to our current problems.

V. Though this course deals primarily with human-domesticate interactions over the past 10,000 years, we need to reach back farther than that to appreciate what it is that is so special about these past 10 millennia.

VI. Our ancient ancestors were effective group hunters and harried some large mammal and bird species to extinction.

VII. Then, about 10,000 years ago, at several different locations on several continents, some fundamental changes began to take place. People went from hunting, gathering, foraging, and fishing to actively producing their own food.

VIII. One hypothesis for these multiple origins is that in each place, some humans found themselves in particularly rich environments for hunting and foraging and therefore began to settle in a single encampment close to their sources of food.

IX. It is clear that without domestication and agricultural food production, humans could not have lived sedentary lifestyles in permanent settlements for long. Without these settled communities, humans would not have attained the population densities and specializations of labor needed to start the journey toward civilization.

Suggested Reading:

Maisels, *The Emergence of Civilization*, chap. 2.
Smith, *The Emergence of Agriculture*, chap. 1.

Questions to Consider:

1. How many reasons can you offer for why human populations began to expand in the Neolithic?

2. If civilization depended upon the development of food production, can hunting-foraging people ever be considered truly civilized? If so, how?

3. Can you offer any explanations for why large animals went almost completely extinct in North and South America but did not disappear in Europe, Eurasia, or Africa?

Lecture One—Transcript
Man the Domesticator

Hello, I'm Gary Sojka and this course is the story of the interplay of man and the plants, animals, and microbes domesticated along the way from our hunting and foraging past to the modern, civilized world. In this course, we'll explore the role that domestication of other creatures played in the greatest transition our species has ever undergone: the change from hunting, fishing, gathering, and scavenging—food procuring, if you will—to becoming a food producer. Our agricultural food-production practices, based on those domestications, set us apart from the other animals on this planet and put us on the path to our current sedentary, civilized way of life. Before that point—before the transition to agricultural food production—we obtained our nourishment like virtually every other animal on the planet: We simply fed on what was available to eat in the environment. This course will be an effort not only to recount many of the steps leading to domestication and the impact those domestication events had on the development of complex, civilized societies, it will also provide context—the back story, if you will—for a number of present-day issues ranging from nutrition and animal rights to population pressure, new medical advances, territorial disputes, and even maybe climate change.

By necessity, this course will need to be very multidisciplinary, delving into subjects and approaches typically associated with subjects such as anthropology, archaeology, history, sociology, geography, ecology, evolution, botany, certainly there's going to be some microbiology, genetics, agronomy, molecular biology, and we might even touch some philosophy. Obviously, then, this series of lectures will not be confined to any of those traditional disciplines, but rather will draw upon all of them to build an appreciation of the essential role the process of domestication has played in the development of civilization. We'll discuss how domestication opened the door to agricultural-food production, which in turn made it possible for civilizations to develop. In other words, to use a phrase often employed by my colleagues in physics, domestication was necessary but not sufficient to the development of human civilization. In other words, if you didn't have those domestications, society and civilization wouldn't have developed as it has; but, of course, there are other things involved, I don't want to overstate the case. What I'm saying, then, is that civilization could not have arisen in the way that it did without animal and plant domestication, but there were other things and we know that; we will not focus on them in this course.

There has been increasing interest in this subject—this subject of the beginnings of agriculture—in recent years, though it's not a brand new idea. Rousseau was asking questions about the "natural" or non-civilized man over 250 years ago. Recent decades have seen significant progress in work on the origins of agriculture, of course, and domestication; in essence, Rousseau was asking: Was civilization as it developed on Earth really a benefit to man? That is a legitimate question with regard to much of what will be covered here, but I won't presume to provide the answer, just some context to the question. By examining some of the key underpinnings of the development of civilization we may be able to provide a somewhat different way of looking at that question posed by Rousseau over 2 centuries ago. As our own generation ponders the pressing problems of feeding a rapidly expanding human population, climate change, and the question of sustainability of our global food supply, the material covered in this course will provide valuable context for this vital public discourse.

The course will be structured in the following way: In the first few lectures, we'll discuss the theories that archaeologists, anthropologists, and others have been able to construct about the history of the first plant and animal domestications and our transition of species from hunting and gathering to our really more agriculturally based food production leading to civilization. We'll talk about what it really means to be domesticated, and try to make a real distinction between plants and animals that are truly domesticated and those that are merely cultivated or tamed. We'll discuss the ways our ancient ancestors went about developing working "partnerships" and establishing a kind of codependency with a number of plants and animals. We'll illustrate how these practices led to our gaining a degree of control over nature and also look into the impact that this increasing influence over parts of the natural world has had on the physical environment.

In the next section, then, of this course, we will explore the history of the domestication of some key plants and animals. Obviously, in a course of this length it will not be possible to give an exhaustive presentation of all the important and interesting plant and animal domestications that have taken place, but I will try to pick illustrative examples employing familiar and interesting organisms to give a sense of the value and the limitations of the practice of domesticating other life forms. From there, we will discuss the way human activities have moved plants, animals, and microbes to new habitats where some have done remarkably well. For example, we're going to such interesting items as the way certain iconic plant types actually found their way to localities that were greatly affected by their presence. We'll explore the way tomatoes came to Italy and potatoes got to Ireland. We'll also look into some interesting animal translocations as well; in so doing, we'll look into such topics as the way horses and cattle found their way to the Americas. Using a few key individuals as examples, we'll talk about the way that agricultural practice grew in importance, how it helped foster population growth and actually determine the fate of nations and how its practice became progressively more systematic and ultimately scientific. Some of these examples may seem surprising, for I will draw my subjects in several cases from outside the world of agriculture or science.

The course will also include a discussion of some new and exciting ways that cutting edge techniques and approaches in the sciences are building on centuries of progress in refining the management of domesticates in order to improve the quality, extent, and the length of human life. We'll also discuss the impacts that new science and technology are having on food production and agricultural practice. Consideration will also be given to benefits and challenges presented as an integrated, global food-production enterprise takes on the challenge of feeding a population that has now reached something in the neighborhood of 6.5 billion people and is continuing to expand without any serious signs of slowing that expansion. We will consider the impacts it is having on climate, water supply, and the condition of the land and the oceans. We'll also look at some novel and new ways that domesticates can be employed in the chemical and pharmaceutical industry to produce products that would be exceedingly difficult to make without such assistance from another life form. Finally, an effort will be made to show how the material in this course dealing with our interaction with our domesticates helps inform the current discussion concerning the very future of our species.

Though I will follow a rough chronological structure, beginning with the Neolithic transformation from food procuring to food producing and ending with our present challenges of feeding an enormously expanded population in a sustainable way, no attempt will be made to actually catalogue or enumerate in a systematic way all the achievements and milestones that occurred between the first domestication events and our efforts at engineering solutions to our current problems. Of course, I will need to limit the number of specific domesticates and our interaction with them to a few key examples as I just mentioned. Among those examples will be some very familiar organisms, but we will also look into the contributions of some creatures that you may not at first have thought of as domesticates, but which do, on reflection, neatly fit the definition of a domesticate that we will develop in this course. It will also be necessary to leap significant portions of time since we'll be trying to highlight some of the most important and intriguing aspects of a story that has been about 10 millennia in the making.

Anyone undertaking to teach such a course would undoubtedly be greatly influenced by his or her own experience and training. Thus, it's probably of some value to take a moment to talk about my own training and background and why I'm drawn to such an interdisciplinary subject at this rather late point in my life. It may at first seem unusual to you that a person with my kind of formal training that I have had would be drawn to such a subject, but as the course unfolds I hope you'll come to understand how the various aspects of my background come together around this subject.

My formal training is in microbial genetics and microbial biochemistry and metabolism, and I've also worked in the field of and bioenergetics. Certainly, none of those fields seem particularly close to the subject matter that I've just said this course will cover. But as I transitioned from research and teaching in these areas to a long career in university and higher education administration including chairmanships, deanships, presidencies, and rolls on commissions and governing and accrediting boards, I began to become increasingly interested in a number of disciplines related more to my youthful experiences in farming and agribusiness than to my past interests in laboratory-based research. In recent years, I've been attempting to actually meld my scientific training and experience with hands-on management of an endangered breeds conservation enterprise. For me, this has been a transformative experience.

By going back to the land, as it were, and engaging in the breeding and management of a group of domesticates, I began to realize just how different the demands and expectations were on a person engaged in such activities from those I had experienced in my earlier years. Those animals and crops were not really on my clock; rather, I found that I was on theirs. As this realization began to sink in, I began to ponder the long path our species has traveled from its first efforts at domestication and food production to our present integrated, technologically-dependent civilization. This global village interconnected with rapid, real-time communication capacities grew from such domestication events, but in just a few millennia became something quite different from a small encampment with a few crops and a few animals associated with it. It was from these realizations and experiences that the desire to teach a course of this kind and to share some of my experiences and insights was born. In giving this course, I'll try to use my formal, academic training and background in science, but I'll also try to bring in the perspective of one who has experienced and is living a different sort of life.

I am an active farmer; I'm engaged in growing crops and in a conservation breeding and maintenance program of flocks of endangered sheep and chickens. Now please note, I'm not saying that chickens and sheep, per se, are endangered; not at all. Rather it is some historic, heritage breeds that are endangered and in need of conservation. Thus, you can expect this course to provide some understanding of what is meant by the term "breed" and why that is so important. Along the way, as an agriculturist, I've served as the President of the American Livestock Breeds Conservancy and the Philadelphia Society for Promoting Agriculture. So I think you can see this will be a tale told by one who is an academic research scientist, but who has also had his hands up inside a struggling ewe trying to assist her in a breech birth and who continues to lug hay and grain to animals knee deep in the snows of a Pennsylvania winter. Mine is admittedly an unusual perspective on this subject, but one that I hope you will come to feel is wholly appropriate to a subject that is at once technical and science-based, but which is also as familiar and practical as the items on your dinner plate or the shoes on your feet.

Though this course deals primarily with human/domesticate interactions over the past 10,000 years, we need to reach back farther than that to appreciate what it is that is so special about these past 10 millennia. Even though anatomically modern humans have been on this planet for about 200,000 years, our story will commence about 10,000 years ago in what is called the Neolithic period, the last part of the so-called ice age, as the glaciers of that last ice age were receding as a result of the most recent mega climatic change. By the end of the Mesolithic Period, the time just before the Neolithic, our kind had spread from its point of origin in Sub-Saharan Africa into every continent save Antarctica. These people had the use of fire and were adept at tool making. The tools were stone, of course, but also undoubtedly employed wood, bone, animal sinew, and other soft materials that simply did not preserve well in what are now archaeological sites, leaving behind the characteristic stone scrapers, mauls, hatchets, arrow heads, and spear points.

These ancient ancestors of ours were making, and thus presumably appreciating, art, and they had rudimentary social structures that held together extended family hunting and gathering groups. They were also very likely spiritual beings that did practice ritual burial and possibly some form of religion. They were effective group hunters and had by this time harried some of the large mammal and bird species to absolute extinction. A combination of hunting, climate change, and what is called hyperdisease—that's a kind of concatenation of a number of infectious diseases and physical disorders and maladies—and these things combined and taken together had eliminated all but just a tiny number of animal species larger than 100 pounds from North America, they'd greatly reduced the number of such animals in South America, and eliminated some large species from Europe, Eurasia, and Africa by the end of this Mesolithic Period.

Then, about 10,000 years ago, at several different locations actually on several continents some fundamental changes began to take place. These transforming events occurred earlier in some locations than in others, but the remarkable thing is that within just a few thousand years of each other, groups of people began an entirely new lifeway. These people went from hunting, gathering, foraging, and fishing to actively producing their own food. This transformation has been called the Neolithic Revolution, but, of course, that term can be misleading. It was not some sort of "eureka" or one-off event that set people on a new path in each of these points of agricultural origin; rather, it was likely a gradual, multi-generational set of practices employed to increase the abundance of plants that had formerly been gathered and to manage animals that had formerly been hunted. One hypothesis for these multiple origins is that in each place some humans found themselves in particularly rich environments for hunting and foraging and as a consequence reduced their wandering and began to settle for most or all of the year in a single encampment close to their sources of food. As their populations began to grow, they began to stress even the abundant supplies that surrounded them, and they needed to "encourage" more yield from the plants and animals on which they now depended. Note that if this hypothesis turns out to be the correct model for how our ancient, prehistoric ancestors made the conversion to being food producers rather than food procurers, it will mean that this move was catalyzed by population pressure and attendant food limitations.

Just to demonstrate how challenging it can be to construct accurate models of the way events unfolded thousands of years ago when there were no living eyewitnesses, no written records, and no hieroglyphs or carvings to decipher, I will bring up an additional piece of information that is relevant to this issue. First of all, please remember that this is a science-based course, and we will say often: Science is self-correcting. When better data appears or better explanations are offered, the accepted models can change. There is work going on at an archaeological site in Turkey that may have a profound effect on our understanding of the pressures or opportunities that drew our early ancestors to the practice of food production. At this site, large stone objects have been unearthed that appear to be monumental objects of worship of some sort. What is fascinating is that these large stones are just too big, and the construction too complex, to fit nicely into our former conception of what hunter-gathers were capable of; yet these objects are dated to a time before it was thought that agriculture had reached this region. What could be the explanation?

One suggestion (and it's a suggestion) is that groups of hunting-gathering people converged at this special, today we might call it holy, site—it is a little bit of an elevated plain—and jointly constructed these monuments. That, of course, increased the population density in the immediate area long enough for the monuments to be fashioned and placed. Even though food was probably abundant in the region for hunting and gathering, this temporary influx of people camped out for the duration stressed the food supply to the extent that some attempt to increase food availability in the immediate region began. Sure enough, some early evidence has emerged suggesting that there were some crude attempts at growing food very near the site at about the time the construction was going on. Interesting? Yes. Compelling? No, not really; but such is science. But given time and continued interest by scientists and committed laypersons around the world, these answers will eventually be forthcoming. Also, please note, that though slightly different from the example that I gave earlier, it was a short-term food limitation that is the catalyst in this model for pushing people into producing food.

As mentioned, domestication of plants and animals, an essential step in real agricultural food production, may at first have occurred incidentally and inadvertently. That is, some of the earliest and most useful domesticates may have been pre-adapted to domestication in the absence of any conscious effort by people to accomplish the domestication. We will have much more to say about this later in the course. It is clear that without domestication and agricultural food production, a sedentary lifestyle in permanent settlements would not have been possible for long, and without settled communities, the population densities, specializations of labor, and tasks needed to start the journey toward civilization would not have been attained. That subject will also be revisited in detail in a later lecture.

So, in essence, this will be a course that attempts to connect our unique capacities as domesticators with the rise of civilization. I will try to make the case that we have, in a sense, "partnered" with a number of other species—plants, animals, and microbes—for mutual benefit, and that jointly we and our domesticates have done remarkably well for the past 10 millennia; so well, in fact, that we have profoundly changed the balance of organisms on the planet and have begun to have significant impacts on the physical as well as the biological environment.

When we approach our next lecture, we're going to discuss the actual process of domestication and explore some of the hypotheses concerning the ways our ancient hunting-gathering ancestors began a kind of mutualistic symbiosis with a number of plants and animals, and by so doing began to exert control over nature rather than just living in nature, a practice with both positive and negative consequences that each generation—our own most notably—must confront. You will hear me use that word "mutualistic" over and over in this course. Later, I'll take the time to define the term more carefully; but it is something that I believe very strongly, both as a biologist and as a farmer. If you can't see how domestication benefits the domesticate at this point, please ponder this issue 'til we meet again. Here's the question: If domestication was not a benefit to chickens, how did they get to be the most numerous and abundant bird on the planet, and how did they attain a wider distribution than any other bird species?

That's an interesting question; obviously, in this course I'm going to answer it for you, and I think you probably already have the clue you need. But I think you can tell from this introduction what kind of a course this is going to be. It's not a course like one that I have ever offered before; it's not something in which I got my Ph.D., did my research, and am now enlightening my students. It's not a course like I've ever given, it's not a course like I've ever taken; it's one that is put together by 2 parallel interests that converge around this central issue in the development of civilization. It comes from my passion for animals, my involvement with them, my understanding of the cellular and molecular structures that make them work, and a desire to assist other people to appreciate that understanding this connection between the domesticates and the civilization in which we live will be critical to answering some of the key questions in front of us right now and that will determine, ultimately, the fate of our species. We'll see you next time with the answer to the chicken question.

Lecture Two
The Beginnings of Domestication

Scope:

Plants and animals in the wild are shaped by natural selection. Of the myriad species that have come in contact with *Homo sapiens sapiens* since its appearance around 200,000 years ago, only a small fraction have been domesticated. Human activity produced domesticates that were genetically and phenotypically distinct from their wild progenitors. The presence of these domesticates made possible the shift to agricultural food production.

Outline

I. Plants, animals, and microbes are susceptible to environmental pressures and are shaped by natural selection.

II. Let's look at seed plants growing in the wild and a few of the traits that might have some bearing on their survivability. These traits are the result of generations of natural selection.

   A. Seeds are surrounded by a coat that can vary in thickness, toughness, and resistance to chemical disruption or desiccation.

   B. Since plants are not capable of locomotion, they require some form of dispersal mechanism to spread over the landscape. Some plants have coevolved with animal partners to help in this task.

   C. In the wild, seeds should be just the right size to optimize reproduction.

   D. There is genetic heterogeneity in wild plants with regard to seed germination. Seeds can germinate synchronously (all in the first available growing season) or asynchronously (some in the first and some in subsequent growing seasons).

III. Animals also show significant genetic heterogeneity in wild populations.

   A. Avoidance of predators (flight response) can aid survivability.

   B. Speed, stealth camouflage, and weapons (such as teeth, claws, and stingers) can help fend off predators or capture prey.

C. Armor of various kinds and group defense tactics can also help fend off predators.

D. Resistance to parasites favors some variants.

E. Natural selection favors animals that can reproduce effectively.

IV. The appearance of modern humans created a different set of environmental pressures and opportunities for plants, animals, and microbes in their immediate environment.

V. Early hunter-gatherers similarly created new sets of pressures and opportunities for the animals in their immediate environments.

VI. It is imperative that we make a clear distinction between truly domesticated animals and tamed animals.

VII. It would be hubris to assume that human beings have the capacity to domesticate any plant, animal, or microbe that we wish. In this course, we repeatedly make the point that domesticates often meet us halfway on the road to domestication.

A. Plants that we have been unable to domesticate include breadfruit, ginseng, morels, and truffles.

B. Animals that we have been unable to domesticate include gazelles, elephants (who are work partners but not domesticates), and some performing animals (tigers, seals, and bears).

VIII. So what is it that causes us to consider a plant, animal, or microbe a domesticate?

A. It must be maintained by, and to at least some degree dependent on, humans.

B. It must have undergone sufficient genetic change that it is both genetically and phenotypically distinct from wild progenitors.

C. It should have some characteristic deemed by the domesticator to be of value to him or her.

IX. What are some of the relationships between domesticated plants and animals and their wild progenitors?

A. Domesticated animals tend to be smaller than their wild progenitors.

B. Many domesticated animals exhibit neoteny. This is marked in cats, dogs, and swine.

C. Most domesticated animals are much more tolerant of humans than their wild progenitors are—making them easier and safer to handle and allowing successful breeding in close proximity to humans.

D. Some plants can revert quickly to wild status, and some animals can exist in a feral state. To some degree, this reversion to weeds and feral animals can be dependent on gene flow between wild types and domesticates.

X. Domestication set us apart from other animals and probably even other humanoids or protohuman primates. It was essential in our transformation from hunter-gatherers to food producers.

XI. Another major and recurring theme in this course is that our domestication of plants and animals is a mutualistic symbiosis.

Suggested Reading:

Hancock, *Plant Evolution*, chaps. 6–7.

Smith, *The Emergence of Agriculture*, chaps. 2–3.

Questions to Consider:

1. What is gained by employing a variety of approaches and techniques when investigating prehistoric events such as the shift from food procurement to food production?

2. Why is it easier to determine the origins of some domesticated plants and animals than others?

3. If we are in a mutually beneficial "partnership" with our domesticates, what benefits do they derive from the association?

Lecture Two—Transcript
The Beginnings of Domestication

Hello, and welcome back. The story of the domestication of plants, animals, and microbes by human beings—what we're calling the human factor—really began prior to the appearance of modern humans on the scene; that is, the proper conditions had to be established in the natural world prior to the participation of humans in the process. A naturally-occurring phenomenon essential to the process is the ability of all populations to adapt genetically over time to changing conditions. This phenomenon is called natural selection. In this lecture, we will briefly review what we mean by "natural selection"; that is, the hereditary response populations make to environmental pressures resulting in the most fit collection of genetic types for the given conditions. It's something that populations, not individuals, respond to. This is a critical point and must be understood, then, from the outset; and all naturally occurring populations of organisms tend to exhibit a significant amount of genetic heterogeneity, making it possible to respond by natural selection to new pressures and opportunities.

Domestication, it turns out, is a 2-way street with natural selection playing an important role, and then followed by conscious, self-aware human activity finishing off the process. It is that human factor that has resulted in a wide array of domesticates—plants, animals, and microbes—that are both genetically and phenotypically different from their wild progenitors. We'll talk briefly about the relationship between the hunter-gatherer and what were likely the first 2 domesticates, one plant and one animal. As methods improve and more information is gathered, new theories and models have arisen to describe these critical events in human history, so we will be discussing our present understanding of the situation. But as with all scientific understandings, as we pointed out last time, it should be kept in mind that what we think we know today is subject to revision in the face of new information or better explanations.

As we said, prior to any involvement by human beings, plants, animals, and microbes in nature are susceptible to environmental pressures and are shaped by natural selection. To illustrate that point, I'm going to just give you a very hypothetical little scenario with no particular details; but I just want to make sure we're understanding how natural selection can shape a population by essentially selecting preexisting types. Natural selection doesn't cause the changes; it selects already-existing types and allows them to become predominant. Here's the little story: We have a group of herbivorous animals, prey animals, living in a given environment. They're shaped by natural selection: they have predators, and they have food sources; that's shaping the distribution of one trait. We'll look at just one trait: the size of the individuals in the population. Most of them are gathered around the middle, but there are some that are quite a bit larger and some that are quite a bit smaller and gradations in between; a standard curve of distribution. Now something happens: A new predator comes on the scene, and he is big, he is vicious, and he likes these little prey animals. He is so big and vicious that being larger than the norm provides absolutely no advantage; you could be bigger than the normal, but you still can't fight this guy off. Being the normal size also doesn't help you, because that's what he's after.

But it turns out that the littlest ones in the population can hide better, and this big, vicious predator doesn't find them. So after a few generations, what has happened to the size of the population of the pretty animals? It's smaller, because these little animals have become the norm, they've found their niche, and they've grown up to be the predominant variety. What were the salient features that made that little example work? There had to be substantial heterogeneity in the population which allowed for some to survive in the new circumstances. It was then the new prevailing conditions that determined which genetic variant of the population ultimately predominated and which ones died out or became extinct. Environmental changes giving rise to new pressures and opportunities select for the variants best suited to these conditions, and they become the predominant type.

Let's turn our attention now to seed plants growing in the wild and look at a few of their traits that might have some bearing on their survivability; we're just talking about plants living in the wild. These traits would be the result of generations of natural selection always working toward making the most fit combination of genetic traits the most prevalent or the norm in the population. Look at one trait first: seed coats. They can differ in character. Seeds are surrounded by a coat that can vary in thickness, toughness, its resistance to chemicals and other disruptions, or desiccation. In a natural setting it is not hard to imagine that a seed coat that is reasonably thick and tough would provide a degree of survivability to the seed and thus might be favored by natural selection. Let's look at another trait: Since plants are not capable of locomotion, they require some form of dispersal mechanism in order to spread over the landscape. Some plants have coevolved with animal partners to help in this task. Various kinds of burrs that can cling to your hair, or your skin, or your sweat socks deliver seeds to new, distinct, distant locations. Also, attractive food surrounding a seed can encourage animals to carry the seeds away and deposit them in different places.

Did you ever wonder, for example, how oak trees manage to get to the top of hills if they reproduce by acorns that roll down hills? That's their way of doing it. Acorns are surrounded by food that's attractive to squirrels, and what do squirrels do with their food? They pick it up, they run to someplace that they know about, dig a little hole, plant the seed, and cover it back up. They plan to come back and get it later. They can go uphill or downhill; doesn't matter, they're animals. Some of the squirrels will go uphill with these acorns and plant them, and if, by chance, that squirrel happens to get bumped off by an automobile or caught by a dog, he's not going to go back up there and dig out his acorns, and he has in effect planted an oak tree on a hilltop. Other methods of dispersion are things like those little whirligigs that you see falling off of maple trees. They carry the seeds away from the base of the tree. Think about things like coconuts floating on the water delivering seeds to different islands. Plants can use a number of those mechanisms.

Finally, among the grasses—and they're important in this course— it is common for the seeds to be attached to the stem by a brittle rachis that shatters upon contact or mild agitation, dispersing the seeds away from the parent plant. That would be the form of the plant that would be favored, one that would kick the seeds out. As was the case with seed coats, natural selection, then, would be expected to favor those plants that had traits which would enhance survivability and expansion, thus it would be expected that successful plants in nature would have developed effective dispersal mechanisms for their seeds.

In the wild, seeds should be just exactly the right size to optimize reproduction. Seeds that are too small may not have adequate food storage, coat thickness, or whatever in order to provide good survivability. But on the other hand, seeds take a lot of energy to make; and making seeds that are larger than necessary would be wasteful, or it might even be making a seed that's too big to disperse easily and these traits would likely be selected against by natural selection. There is also genetic heterogeneity in wild plants with regard to seed germination. Seeds can germinate synchronously—that is, all in the first available growing season—or they can germinate asynchronously with some germinating in the first growing season and others waiting around and germinating in subsequent seasons. If you've ever tried to eradicate weeds from your garden or your lawn, you have likely witnessed asynchronous germination of weed seeds; you think you get them all one year, they're back the next. Asynchronous germination is a way for a plant to "hedge its bets" with regard to finding a good growing season.

Animals, like plants, show significant genetic heterogeneity in wild populations. Natural selection works on animals, as we have pointed out in our little hypothetical example, to select for the most fit phenotype, and its corresponding genotype. I've used that word twice; let me just quickly point out what we mean by "genotype" and "phenotype." The "genotype" refers to the plants' genes or genetic material, its DNA, that which it received directly from its parents. The phenotype is what happens when the genes are expressed into form or function; so the form and function of the creature is its phenotype, it's a result of the expression of the genotype. Animals, like plants have a number of features that help determine long-term survivability or fitness in the surroundings. In natural populations, each of those features will show significant genetic variation.

Let's look at a few such features. One is avoidance of predators, what we call flight response. Obviously, if a predator is nearby the animals that respond to that more quickly and flee more quickly are probably going to be favored by natural selection. What other things could we think about that would be favored by selection? Speed, stealth, camouflage, weapons—weapons like teeth, claws, stingers, etc.—but those things can also be used to fend off predators and to capture prey. Some of these things could be used either way. Some animals use armor of various kinds to provide defense, and we can think of those creatures—turtles, armadillos, shellfish, and so on—and they use that to fend off predators. Also, sometimes there are behavioral mechanisms for defending: Musk oxen will from a circle when a predator's around with all the big animals with big horns facing out and all the more vulnerable animals on the inside. Whales will do it just the other way around: They'll form a circle with all the heads on the inside and those big, flopping tails—which are quite dangerous—on the outside, a way to defend against predators. Natural selection, almost by definition then, favors animals that can reproduce effectively.

The appearance of modern humans created a different set of environmental pressures and opportunities for the plants, animals, and microbes in their immediate environment. Hunter-gatherers—probably inadvertently at first—created localized conditions that impacted a number of plant characteristics, creating new pressures and new opportunities, thus altering the plant populations through natural selection. Some variants were favored and some were negatively impacted. By selectively harvesting seeds that were easy to gather they inadvertently took back to their camp variants that had poor mechanical dispersal mechanisms. Think about this: Here's a hunter-gatherer coming up the hill; he wants to gather seeds from a grass. Most of the grasses, when he gets near it, just the rustling causes the rachis to fracture and the seeds are all over the ground and he's crawling around trying to find them; but there will be a few that have the seeds all bundled up at the top making a real easy pick, and he gets all the seeds without having to bend down. That's a disadvantage in the wild, but the human being is inadvertently now, as he takes these seeds back to his camp, enriching the area around his camp for that characteristic. For reasons having to do, then, with ease of preparation these early modern humans may have selectively gathered seeds that were large—maybe larger than optimum—and had relatively thin or tender seed coats. Again, they would take a disproportionate number of these seeds back to their settlement or camp. By so doing, they were providing a new set of selective pressures and opportunities on these plant variants, and they were doing it without knowing what they were doing.

Once our ancient ancestors began to appreciate that some of the plants that they found around their settlements had properties that they valued as a result of their inadvertent selections of seeds, they began to place negative pressure on competing weeds by cultivating the soil and planting the seeds they preferred. Preparation of the soil by scratching the surface or later by plowing took away the advantage offered by a thick or resistant seed coat, because now it's new conditions; it diminished any advantage that plants had in competing with weeds because the human beings were taking the weeds out. In a natural environment, of course, asynchronous germination is favored, but in this environment synchronous germination is favored because the human beings would select some of these seeds and plant them in the next year; so it was useful to come up in the first year. Thus, a combination of inadvertent and directed human activities changed the selective pressure enough to generate plants that were sufficiently different from their progenitors, both genetically and phenotypically, to be considered different plants; they were, in effect, domesticated.

The first domesticated plant was probably the bottle gourd. Interestingly, it was not a food source, but a utility carrier that could transport other seeds, food items, and possibly even liquids. The wild progenitor had a thin skin, but early hunter-gatherers soon selected for harder-skinned variants because they could hold more materials dependably. After only a few generations, these "domesticated" bottle gourds had skins that were much tougher than the wild type. The great utility of this plant resulted in its spread around much of the globe carried by hunter-gatherers on their way out of Africa to colonize much of the globe.

Early hunter-gatherers similarly created new sets of pressures and opportunities for the animals in their immediate environment. Dog provides an excellent example. Zoologists have postulated the existence of a wolf variant that they now call "protodog." It may have had a less well-developed flight response than typical wolves; it may have been less effective as a hunter, and possibly was a bit smaller in stature. Such an animal, though arising naturally in the population was at a distinct disadvantage in the habitat of the wild wolf pack, and thus was probably only an insignificant component of the wolf population. It may have even been driven out of the pack by the other wolves. But when man came on the scene, he created a zone around his place of activity that favored this creature. Why? Man makes scraps when he eats and he tosses them around, and these protodogs were probably very good scavengers, so they were eating—as dogs do today—out of the garbage dumps of human beings. But people were doing something else: People were also suppressing the predator population immediately around them; as they protected themselves and their encampments, they provided a zone of protection for these protodogs. Since protodog probably had a poorly developed flight response, he was rather tolerant of the people being around; he would come up close to them, and they could begin to have some kind of interplay. Finally, protodog was probably not a real competitor for man in terms of being a hunter, so he was tolerated; and the relationship between man and dog probably came about that way with dogs meeting us more than halfway through that protodog variant. If a man just went into a wolf pack and pulled one out and said, "I'm going to start a domesticated line," good luck.

At this point, it is imperative that we make a clear distinction, then, between a truly domesticated animal and any number of tamed animals. Let me illustrate this with a story from my own childhood. When I was quite young, my dad brought home a young raccoon, a baby raccoon, and he said, "This would be fun for Gary to have in the house," and it was. We were such an original family, we named him Ricky; we gave him apples, and if you know about raccoons he would wash his apple in his food dish and he would eat it very neatly, and he had nice habits. We had a fenced yard, he would go out and do the things he needed to do, and he would actually come back in because he knew where his food dish was, his blanket was, and so on. He was quite nice to be around, but my mother was getting worried because his claws were growing and his teeth were going. One day while I was sitting on the floor with Ricky watching television and chewing gum, Ricky's little hand darted into my mouth, grabbed the chewing gum, and my mother banished him. Here's the important point: When we took Ricky out to the woods and let him go, he was really not at any disadvantage; he was not a domesticated animal, he was a wild animal and he fit very nicely into that environment. He was genetically and phenotypically no different than any other raccoon.

It would be hubris to assume that human beings have the capacity to domesticate any plant, animal, or microbe that they wish. Repeatedly in this course, we'll make the point that the domesticates often meet us halfway on the road to complete domestication. We have already provided several examples of that in several of our little stories. Think of the domestication of some seed plants or the domestication of the dog. Additional evidence for that claim comes from the observation that we have encountered some notable failures and some only marginal successes in our attempts to domesticate some plants and animals. Among the plants are ginseng, morels, and truffles; try as we might, we really don't do very well at domesticating them. In the animal world, gazelles; we know that the ancient Egyptians tried to domesticate gazelles, no luck. Elephants live among people, they are good work partners; they are not genetically or phenotypically different from the elephants living outside the human situation, they are not domestic. A number of performing animals people have tried to domesticate—things like tigers, seals, bears, etc.—but we must always keep in mind that these aren't domesticated animals, they are wild animals, hence somewhat unpredictable as we have seen from some of the rather horrendous accidents that have happened when people have taken these tamed but not domesticated animals for granted.

So what is it that causes us to consider a plant, animal, or even a microbe a domesticate? First, it must be maintained by humans, and to at least some degree be dependent on humans. It must have undergone sufficient genetic change that it is both genetically and phenotypically distinct from its wild progenitors. It should have some trait or characteristic deemed by the domesticator to be of value to him or her. Although the earliest examples of domestication may lead back almost 35,000 years—that is, the bottle gourds and the dog—the bulk of crop and livestock domestications did not begin until about 10,000 years ago. But it was not really until the 19th century that a cousin of Charles Darwin, Francis Galton, actually proposed a formal definition for what is meant by a domesticate. We will discuss his 6 characteristics in some detail in a later lecture.

What are some of the relationships between domesticated plants and animals and their "wild" progenitors? These are not hard and fast rules devoid of exception, but generally, domesticated animals tend to be smaller than their wild progenitors. This is certainly true for cattle, sheep, and swine, all of which are smaller than their presumed wild progenitors. On the other hand, domesticated plants tend to be larger, on average, than their progenitors. Also, many domesticated animals exhibit a trait known as neoteny; that is, the maintenance of juvenile characteristics all the way to the level of sexual maturity. You really see this in swine when you note that even a big domesticated boar does not have a snout and tusks like a wild boar. Most domesticated animals are much more tolerant of man, too, than their wild progenitors are, making them easier and safer to handle and allowing successful breeding in close proximity to humans. Some plants can revert back rather quickly to wild status acting as weeds, and some but not all animals can exist in the feral state. To some degree, this reversion to weeds and feral animals can be dependent on gene flow between wild types and domesticates. In some cases, such gene flow is common and in other cases it's almost non-existent. In the case of turkeys, it would be very common; in the case of corn, not very likely.

Domestication, then, set us apart from other animals—there's one minor exception in the ant world of leaf cutter ants, and we will not worry about those—and probably even other humanoids or proto-humans did not domesticate other creatures, that's something left to modern humans. Domestication was essential in our transformation from hunter-gatherers, as all other animals are, to food producers. It made possible the sedentary lifestyle with fixed settlements that we will discuss in the next lecture and it opened the door to the development of civilization. Thus, it can be said that the practice of domestication was an essential, if not sufficient, precursor to the advent of civilization.

Another major and recurring theme in this course is that our domestication of plants and animals is a kind of mutualistic symbiosis. In order to fully understand the importance of this from a biological perspective we'll need to consider the following terms: First, let's talk about symbiosis itself. When a biologist uses that term, he is simply talking about 2 different organisms living together. Often in common parlance, we mean something different by that: When we say "symbiosis," I think we are frequently implying "synergy"; that's not what we mean here, it simply means "2 organisms living together." That concept—organisms living together—can break down into at least 3 distinct types of symbiosis. The first one we'll talk about is parasitism. That's a situation where one of the partners clearly benefits and the other is clearly damaged. That will become important in this course because we're going to talk about domesticated animals and their resistance to parasites; for example, internal parasites will actually draw blood from animals, draw them down, make them sick, and ultimately kill them but the parasite benefits.

Commensalism is the situation where one partner benefits but the other is totally unaffected. The classic example of that is a tree on which is growing a staghorn fern. The fern benefits from being able to anchor itself on the tree and get in the right position, but the tree is totally unaffected. The third kind of symbiosis is mutualism. That's the kind we're talking about when we talk about domestication, because in that kind of symbiosis, both partners should benefit; and when biologists talk about "benefit" they usually only are really talking about not whether the animal's happy or the plant looks good, they're talking about the numbers in the population, whether they're going up and remaining strong, and the distribution of the organism. Therein you have the answer to the chicken question posted in the last lecture.

It is interesting to note that after living as food procurers for almost 190,000 years, in one of the greatest revolutions in the history of our species agricultural, food-producing communities began to spring up around the globe within just a few thousand years of each other. As we'll see in the next lecture, we became increasingly codependent on a variety of plant and animal species as our settled communities expanded and evolved into cities, city-states, nations, and now ultimately a kind of global food community. This increasing codependence between us and our domesticates is another recurring theme in this course. In the final lectures we will revisit this subject with the intent of making the point that our generation, the one probably least cognizant of our dependence on domesticates of any generation in the last 10,000 years is, in fact, more dependent on the process of domestication than any generation that has gone before.

We'll see you next time.

Lecture Three
The Basis for Settled Communities

Scope:

In this lecture, we look at how early efforts by humans to domesticate plants and animals moved us toward settled communities and closer to the food-producing civilization with which we are familiar.

Outline

I. There is a lot of guesswork involved in piecing together this story.

   A. The biological method developed by Vavilov has provided much information about the origin of domesticated plants.

   B. The archaeological method developed by Robert Braidwood for studies of agricultural origins in the Middle East builds up a model for what occurred based on typical archaeological methodologies.

   C. Isotopic dating provides a method of assigning absolute dates to some materials. The best known and most widely used of these techniques is carbon-14 dating.

II. Modern humans lived as food procurers for about 190,000 of our approximately 200,000-year existence. Then, in one of the greatest transformations in the history of our species, the bulk of the population around the world took up a new lifeway by becoming agricultural food producers.

III. The Stone Age is generally divided into 3 overlapping phases, beginning with the Old Stone Age.

   A. The Paleolithic, or Old Stone Age, is named for the stone tools humans and prehumans used during this period. Well over 95% of the existence of our species was during this period.

   B. The Mesolithic, or Middle Stone Age, varied from location to location. It is distinguished from the previous age by the sophistication of tools and ended with the advent of farming and systematic herding about 5000 years ago.

C. The Neolithic is the part of the Stone Age that will be of greatest interest to us in this course. It correlates roughly with the receding ice sheets at the end of the last ice age and is marked by the beginnings of agricultural food production, the Neolithic Revolution.

IV. It is not known for certain why agricultural practices emerged simultaneously at a number of different sites, but many believe that the primary trigger was climate change.

V. The transition to the agricultural way of life was not always absolute or exclusive. There is evidence that in a number of places, foraging people lived in close proximity to Neolithic food producers.

VI. As the Neolithic Revolution progressed, significant changes came in rapid succession, contributing to the growth in the number of settled communities and the rise in population.

VII. With the rise in settled communities came the rise in technology for agriculture and other aspects of civilized life. Methods and implements had to be developed for preparation of the soil, planting, and harvesting.

VIII. As population densities increased and people began to live in close proximity to their domesticated animals, public health issues took on new significance.

IX. This new way of living also created tensions among individuals and groups that needed to be addressed. In most cases, this was accomplished through the development of some form of legal code.

X. In large part because of the need to control land and technology over time periods extending beyond a single human lifetime, the concepts of patrimony and intergenerational inheritance were developed in these emerging legal codes.

XI. Food producers in settled communities quickly began to displace the previously dominant hunter-gatherer cultures to less hospitable and less desirable habitats, where most of the few remaining food-procuring cultures are found today.

Supplementary Reading:

Bible (King James Version), Genesis 2:7–4:17.

Maisels, *The Emergence of Civilization*, chap. 4.

Questions to Consider:

1. What role would a priestly class be expected to play in food production and distribution?

2. What would be the impact on gender roles as people moved from food procurement to food production?

3. How did state religions come into being as cities grew into states or city-states?

4. Is population increase the cause or the result of the conversion from food procurement to food production?

Lecture Three—Transcript
The Basis for Settled Communities

Welcome. In the last lecture we discussed the genetic heterogeneity of plants and animals that permitted natural selection to occur in the wild. We then discussed the new pressures that human beings put upon plants and animals that resulted in the beginnings of domestication. In this lecture, we're going to talk about how those early domestication efforts between humans, plants, and animals moved us toward settled communities and closer to the food-producing civilization with which we are all so familiar.

There is a lot of guesswork involved in piecing together this story; this early history is very hard to establish definitively. "How do we think we know what we know?" is an important question to raise. Since this is a course dealing with a scientific approach to the study of the domestication events and agricultural practices leading to civilization, we should spend a few minutes discussing the basic approaches that have been employed to piece together the story of the first farmers. We'll start with what is called the "biological method." It was developed by a Russian plant geneticist named Vavilov, and he provided much information about the origin of domesticated plants. Some of the same reasoning can also be applied to animal studies, though Vavilov only really worked with plants. What he did was essentially look for ranges of wild progenitors by using a map—by mapping different specimens that he found—and looking at the genomes of those specimens, and what he was looking for was the spot on the map that had the richest array of different genomes. He deduced that because that array existed, those plants had been there longer, and therefore that was likely the place of origin for the domesticates. We'll return to Vavilov later in this course; he is this sort of tragic character, and we're going to give him some time because he connects somewhat to our time in history.

Another approach, the Archaeological method developed by Robert Braidwood for studies of archaeological origins in the Middle East, builds up a model for what occurred based on typical archaeological methodologies. Various materials can be found throughout what might have been encampments; but, of course, always a very rich source of useful material are middens, or garbage dumps, around these camps where early humans simply tossed things like animal bones or broken tools, and that would really help archaeologists figure out what went on thousands of years ago. Seeds and plant materials can be found associated with all kinds of ancient cooking materials, and that's also filled with clues for what was going on. Bones and teeth of animals can reveal much information. For example, if the species, sex, and age of animals can be determined from such materials—and that is very often the case—it is possible to give a very accurate estimate of the point at which our hunter-gatherer ancestors began to husband and presumably domesticate certain livestock.

Let me explain that a little bit: If you were a hunter-gatherer—if you were just hunting animals and eating them and throwing the bones in your midden or your garbage heap—you would expect a mixture of male/female, young/old because there was no particular rhyme or reason, you were catching what you could catch and killing what you could kill. You might see a preponderance of younger animals and a preponderance of quite a bit older animals because they may have been a little bit weakened or not as able to get away, but there probably wouldn't be much sex difference. But as we look at these middens, you'll see this kind of mixture of bones where there's no particular relationship to age and sex, and all of a sudden, rather abruptly, you start to see a change: Suddenly you see a preponderance of young male bones, and when you find female bones, they're usually from a very old animal. Archaeologists put their finger out and say, "Aha, these people were managing their flocks." Why do they say that? As a sheepherder myself, I can tell you why: These people realized that in the world of sheep—and the same is true with cattle and swine—one male can service a significant number of females making most of the other males (and I'm sorry to say this, fellows) superfluous.

So what happens? You don't want to keep a bunch of superfluous males around. One, they consume food; 2, they fight among themselves and some of them get hurt, and it might be your best one that gets hurt. Three, they're unpleasant to be around very often; they add a level of danger and excitement to herding that isn't there if they aren't there in large numbers. Finally, by narrowing the number of them that you use and carefully picking the very best one you can improve the quality of your flock. When they saw this change in the distribution of male/female, young/old bones in these middens, they said, "Aha, these people have figured it out; they're managing their flocks, and that probably is leading to domestication."

Another important scientific method used is isotopic dating, which provides a method of assigning absolute dates to some materials or samples. The best-known and most widely used of these techniques is carbon-14 dating. Let me just take a second to explain that as well. Carbon exists in the atmosphere in the form of CO_2 mostly in 2 isotopic forms. The predominant one is C12, but there is a radioactive isotope, C14, which makes up a fixed percentage of the carbon in the atmosphere; but C14 is radioactive and it decays, turning into C12. When an animal is growing and it's laying down its bones, carbon is getting put in there into its material, into its body parts, and when the animal dies that process stops and this carbon is trapped in there (no more going in, no more coming out). Over a long period of time, what happens? The C14 continues to decay into C12; so over time, the ratio of C14 to C12 changes. By knowing the exact half life, or the length of time it takes for C14 to decay, you can make very accurate assessments of the age of a sample assuming it contains carbon; but that's often the case in biological materials because we lived in a carbon-based biosphere.

As pointed out earlier, *Homo sapiens sapiens* lived as food procurers for about 190,000 of our approximately 200,000-year existence. Then, in one of these great transformations, the greatest probably in history, our species within only a few thousand years simply changed the bulk of the population and took up a new way of life by becoming agricultural food producers. Let's orient a bit to the time period we're talking about. This is the period often called the Stone Age, because people of the time were adept at making and using stone tools. The Stone Age is generally divided into 3 overlapping phases beginning with the Old Stone Age or the Paleolithic. The dates for these periods are, of course, approximate and differ with geography, coming sooner to some regions than to others. The Paleolithic or Old Stone Age is named for the stone tools humans and pre-humans employed during this period; so some of our non-modern human ancestors or relatives were also living in that period. It encompasses well over 95% of the existence of our species, modern man (*Homo sapiens sapiens*); 95% of our existence was spent in the Paleolithic.

The Mesolithic or Middle Stone Age varied from location to location, of course; and in Europe and the Middle East it was thought to have begun 12,000 to 15,000 years ago and is roughly separated from the Paleolithic by the level of sophistication of the stone tools made by people living in the era. The era is generally considered to have ended with the advent of farming and systematic herding which began—of course, as we've said—at different times in different places. By all accounts, the Mesolithic was over everywhere by about 5000 years ago. The people of this period hunted small creatures, fished, and ate a wide variety of plant materials. There is some evidence they used fire to move animal herds. As the ice sheets receded, these Mesolithic hunter-gatherers began to hunt larger animals that became available to them. They generally had no settled or permanent communities, though there is good evidence that groups of hunter-gatherers in this period often returned to the same encampments at the approximately the same season each year.

We know these people made art in caves and produced decorative or ceremonial objects. Interestingly, evidence shows that the people of this era really were well-nourished and were quite healthy. They were rather large of stature and we think they ate a diet composed of a number of different plants and a variety of animals. In fact, recent studies suggest that these late Mesolithic hunter-gatherers may have been healthier and larger of stature than the farmers that ultimately displaced them. They also generally had better dentition than the early farmers who suffered more tooth decay as a result of their grain-based diets that had higher sugar contents and lower amounts of trace elements. Hunter-gatherers in favorable localities needed to spend only a very small portion of their time in the quest for food. They probably had few material possessions, they did not have to perform much work in order to sustain themselves, and there is little evidence that they suffered much from what we consider communicable disease.

The next period, the Neolithic, is the part of the Stone Age that will be of greatest interest to us in this course. It began at various times in various localities, but generally it is considered to have lasted from about 12,000 to 5000 years ago. It correlates roughly with the receding ice sheets at the end of the last ice age, and is marked by the beginnings of agricultural food production, that so-called "Neolithic Revolution." It marks one of the most profound transitions in the history of our species, because it was at that time that humans began to exert more control over nature by producing rather than hunting and gathering their food. That "revolution" made us different from all the other animals in terms of how we feed. It set the stage for the advent of civilization and placed us squarely on a path we are inexorably following to this very day.

I find the story of the expulsion from the garden in the Book of Genesis interesting in regard to this profound transition from food procuring to food production. What are some of the key elements of the story that lead me to find this so interesting? First, the story may date from about 10,000 to 15,000 years ago in various oral traditions, later in written form. That fairly well matches the period when humans were making the conversion to food production in the Middle East. Let's look briefly at some of the main elements of the story. Before the fall, Adam and Eve were innocent in the garden—read that Earth; garden/Earth—and the garden, or Earth, fed them. They had no clothes—read: material goods and technology—and apparently they did not work. After eating from the tree of the knowledge of good and evil—read there the ability to produce food through domestication of plants and animals and exerting influence on nature—the benefits of the garden were denied Adam and Eve and their descendents. Could this story be interpreted as a metaphor for our change from the food procuring to the agricultural way of life? If so, that tree with the strange name, "the knowledge of good and evil," takes on very special significance for the remainder of this course.

It is not known for certain why agricultural practices emerged at a number of different sites almost simultaneously—that is, if a few thousand years can be considered "simultaneous"—but many believe that the primary trigger was climate change. As those ice sheets receded, more plants began to grow profusely, more game was available, and populations began to settle into favorable places. As their populations grew, these settled communities outstripped the local resources and had to learn to produce food if they were going to be able to stay there.

The transition to the agricultural way of life was not always absolute or exclusive in a given region. There is some evidence that in a number of places foraging people lived in close proximity to Neolithic food producers. There is a growing body of evidence to suggest that the interactions between the Neolithic food producers and their food procuring neighbors, who were still following the old Mesolithic ways, were sometimes violent, even involving acts of ritual cannibalism. In other instances, the interplay between neighboring cultures may have been a bit more benign.

The early Neolithic food producers broke roughly into 2 groups: horticulturists, who cultivated plants for food; and pastoralists, who raised animal herds. We'll talk more about these 2 groups in a later lecture. Of course, there were also the integrated farmers who did both; but it's easy to think about these 2 types. Horticulturalists arose in areas where water supply was available. They undoubtedly supplemented their diets by hunting and fishing. This was not uncommon in Eurasian, Asian, or African regions and in the Americas, where few large animals survived after the ice sheets receded. Committed pastoralists arose in more arid regions of the world, as it were, because it was possible for them to drive their herds to water holes. Undoubtedly they did not subsist exclusively on animal products, but most likely supplemented their diets by foraging and browsing while tending or herding their flocks or herds.

As the Neolithic Revolution progressed, significant changes came in rapid succession that contributed to the growth in the number of settled communities and the rise in population. The actual patterns of conversion to food production from food procurement likely varied from place to place depending on local conditions and past cultural practices of the people involved. The availability of surplus food, the development of specialization in labor, and the resulting organization of manpower that resulted from the formation of settled communities led in many cases to increasing local populations. That, in turn, led to the necessity to produce more food.

It should be noted: Human females in settled, agricultural communities probably produced more children in their lifetimes than their hunting-gathering counterparts. That may seem strange, so let me explain that for a second. We know in our modern world that young women who are committed, sometimes elite athletes actually suppress the number of menses that they experience during the year. We might assume that these hunter-gatherer females, walking and moving all the time and eating this very nice balanced primarily plant diet, were probably quite fit, so they may not have essentially been available to be impregnated as often as their more sedentary counterparts. But even of greater interest is the fact that these hunter-gatherers, because of their diet, had very little access to soft food, so these hunter-gatherer mothers very likely couldn't wean their young away quickly, they had to continue to breastfeed them until they were almost able to operate on their own. That, of course—that lactation—suppressed ovulation, and so a typical hunter-gatherer female might only produce, say, 2 offspring in her life; that would not be the case with the typical female living in one of these settled agricultural communities, and so that added to the growing population pressure in these early settled communities.

When these early agriculturists encountered the problem of an expanding population and the consequent need to produce more food, they had only 2 choices. Those same 2 choices are with us still today; so please attend carefully to this point, it is a major point in this course and we will return to it repeatedly. One way to get more food in an agricultural situation: use the land more efficiently and more intensively. That approach is as old as the first settled agricultural communities, and it remains a major part of our survival strategy to this day. More food could also be produced if more useful land could be attained by preparation or by acquiring it from others; hence, some of these early settled communities became regional powers with hegemonic tendencies in order to control more productive land.

With the rise in settled communities came the rise in technology for agriculture and then other aspects of civilized life. Methods and implements had to be developed for preparation of the soil and for planting and harvesting. Food preparation and food storage required increases in technology. Of course, with surplus food and specialization of labor came increases in technology related to military activities, housing, public works such as roads, religious structures, government buildings, sewers, and granaries just to mention a few. Technology was also employed to produce consumer goods for comfort, grooming, adornment, or aggrandizement. As people became increasingly dependent upon their ability to produce food, they became increasingly dependent on the technologies that supported this way of life. Roughly 5000 years ago there was a marked increase in the development of activities that would result in modern science and technology.

Information about weather, seasons, and growing conditions placed a premium on the study of astronomy. The measurement and division of land required mathematics and geometry. Distribution of food required the development of weights and measures. In the Middle East—and likely in other locals, as well—irrigation was critical to maximizing output of food from the land. This practice not only required careful methods for measuring and dividing land and construction of dams, flood gates, and channels, it also demanded the development of legal codes and methods of enforcement of the laws and rules to maintain order; note again that what we're doing here is exerting more control over nature when we're irrigating. Issues of land ownership probably arose as a result of irrigation, with lands that had water on them more highly desired than lands that had to have water carried in. From these early beginnings arose such concepts as personal, private, and public property—those things don't mean a lot to hunter-gatherers—which began to take on more importance and require more oversight and management. This provides an example of one of the ways that civilization and agriculture based on domestication of plants and animals have been linked from the very beginning.

As population densities increase and people begin to live in close proximity to their domesticated animals, public health issues—something of little concern to widely dispersed hunter-gatherers—began to take on new significance. Zoonotic diseases—diseases communicated from animals to humans under natural conditions—arose and critical population densities were achieved for the establishment and spread of infectious disease. Though attempts were made to ameliorate the effects of these scourges of the settled lifestyle, little progress was made until relatively modern times; and that is not to say that these problems don't represent a continuing threat to human life and health. In fact, the threat of devastating pandemic is always with us and has its roots in these early settled communities where people and livestock cohabited in crowded conditions. In some parts of the world, those conditions persist and that is the principal cause of the almost annual influenza epidemics emanating from Asia and spreading around the world.

This new way of living also created new tensions among individuals and groups that needed to be addressed. In most cases, this was accomplished through the development of some form of legal code or body of civil rules and expectations. Many of these had their origins, as I said before, in the establishment of boundaries and procedures relating to irrigation and agricultural practice. In large part because of the need to control land and technology over time periods extending beyond a single human lifetime, the concepts of patrimony and intergenerational inheritance were developed and addressed in these emerging legal codes. In our own time and on the front pages of our newspapers we see the continuing struggle emanating from ancient decisions and claims played out as modern people continue to wrangle over who has rightful claim to given pieces of land; and I think you're all familiar with those.

Let's quickly review some of the major changes to the way people live resulting from domestication, food production, and the resulting move to a sedentary way of life. The incentive and opportunity for specialized labor definitely increased. The concept of territoriality was enhanced and the concepts of personal, private, and public possessions were refined. Religion became more formalized and tied to the needs of food production and continuance of and cohesiveness of the community. Human diet began to change and become more restricted. Attitudes toward work, leisure, and time began to change. Though there was probably less leisure time per capita in these settled communities than in hunter-gatherer groups where people really didn't work, leisure time and goods were also distributed much more heterogeneously in these settled communities. The concept of ownership and intergenerational inheritance began to take on new importance. There was a heightened need for laws to settle disputes, distribute goods, and resolve issues of ownership. Communicable diseases and public health became major issues. Obviously, all matters of polity are more complex in settled communities than in hunting-foraging groups.

We've talked a lot about the changes that occurred in our communities and to the plants and animals around us; but it is worth noting that this change in lifeway to food production and all that accompanied it brought about some changes in us as well. It is becoming increasingly clear that though we are still very similar physically to those Mesolithic wandering hunter-gatherers, human evolution has not stopped. Over time, our immune systems and other responses to environmental challenge have undergone change. Our vision is likely different, and there may have been subtle changes in skeleton and musculature in response to different selective pressures in this new way of living. It is certainly worth noting and emphasizing that we had nearly 200,000 years as modern humans living like all other animals as food procurers. Natural selection obviously worked on us during that time and on all our pre- or proto-human ancestors. Our "grand experiment" as food producers has been going on for only 5 to 10,000 years. Though we have made some adaptive genetic changes, they are apparently subtle; thus, some of our modern problems dealing with reproductive physiology, nutrition, sleep patterns, and social interaction may emanate from the fact that our lifestyle and way of life is quite different from the one that selected for our present phenotypes. Those are interesting things to keep in mind as we prepare to move into our next lecture.

Despite some of the problems of adjustment just mentioned, in a rather short time—just a few thousand years—food producers in settled communities began to successfully displace the previously dominant hunter-gatherer cultures to less hospitable and less desirable habitats where most of the few remaining food procuring cultures are found today. By A.D. 1500, the vast majority of the people on Earth were sustained by food that was produced by agriculture. In our next lecture, we will discuss the dispersal and spread of early agricultural enterprise around the globe. We'll see you then.

Lecture Four
The Dispersal and Spread of Agriculture

Scope:

In this lecture, we cover a few of the approaches being used to determine the origins of various plant and animal domesticates and to follow the spread of agricultural food production. We then briefly follow the spread of the domesticate-based agricultural lifeway from a few key origin points. By A.D. 1500, this lifeway had become the primary way of nourishing the bulk of the world's population. The hunter-gatherers had become a minority and had been displaced to the margins of the civilized world.

Outline

I. In a matter of only a few thousand years, agriculture had become the dominant way of life around the world. How do we know this, considering we are dealing with a period of time that precedes written records?

   A. The biological approach pioneered by Nikolai Vavilov.

   B. The archaeological approach pioneered by Robert Braidwood of the University of Chicago in the 1940s.

   C. Isotopic direct dating.

   D. Molecular biology techniques.

   E. Historical comparative linguistics.

   F. We gain confidence when different measurements and assumptions give supporting evidence.

II. There are several models, based on the study of archaeological sites, for the way agriculture spread from its various points of origin. It is generally believed that agriculture spread because it was emulated by or imposed upon neighboring peoples.

III. There were at least 7 widely separated sites of primary agricultural origin.

   A. From the Fertile Crescent, agricultural practices moved through Anatolia into Mediterranean Europe and southern Europe, as well as up the Danube to temperate Europe and western Europe.

B. Agriculture also spread eastward from Southwest Asia into eastern Europe, all the way to the Eurasian steppe.

C. Agriculture radiated out from points of origin in East Asia and Southeast Asia to Oceania.

D. The Indian Subcontinent was a site of some initial domestications, but agriculture in this region also blended with that moving east out of Southwest Asia.

E. Though agriculture appears to have spread from Southwest Asia into North Africa fairly early, sub-Saharan Africa may have been an independent focus for its development in the Neolithic.

F. Agriculture also appears to have radiated out from several centers of independent origin in the Americas.

IV. The patterns followed depended on resources available and regional practices of the people adjusting to food production.

A. There were examples of integrated farmers fairly early in the development of agriculture. This was the pattern that developed in the Fertile Crescent.

B. There were likely pastoralists who hunted and fished to supplement their diet. This would have been common in the Americas because of the paucity of domesticated large animals.

C. It was also likely the case that dedicated pastoralists did some browsing or gathering to supplement their diets as they tended their flocks or herds.

D. Horticulturists also supplement their diets with hunting and fishing. This pattern prevails in the modern era: Many of my agricultural neighbors depend on hunting to keep their freezers stocked with meat.

V. Despite evidence that farmers and gathers lived in close proximity, it is undeniable that the food-producing way of life came to dominate.

Suggested Reading:

Bellwood, *First Farmers*, chaps. 1–8.

Chrispeels and Sadava, *Plants, Food, and People*, chap. 6.

Maisels, *The Emergence of Civilization*, chap. 3.

Smith, *The Emergence of Agriculture*, chap. 5.

Questions to Consider:

1. Which mode of food production do you feel came first, pastoralism or horticulture? Would your answer be true in all emerging agricultural societies?

2. If the hunter-gatherer lifestyle has many advantages, why do you suppose food procurers were displaced by food producers so completely in such a relatively short time?

3. What sort of archaeological evidence would you look for to document the spread of early agricultural communities? What other forms of evidence could be useful in documenting the spread of agriculture?

Lecture Four—Transcript
The Dispersal and Spread of Agriculture

Hello, and welcome to this presentation on the spread of agricultural food production around the world. As promised in an earlier lecture, I'll take the next few minutes to cover several of the different scientific approaches that are being used to determine origins of various plant and animal domesticates, and also to follow the spread of agricultural food production from its places of origin to other areas and habitats. Once we have discussed some of these approaches and their applicability to certain questions, we will briefly follow the spread of the domesticate-based, agricultural way of life from a few of the key origin points to other points on the globe. A major theme of this discussion will be the actual patterns that seemed to emerge in our example cases, and when possible we'll try to relate the patterns of spread to the conditions prevailing at that particular time and place.

It's really important to note that by no later than A.D. 1500 the agricultural way of life had essentially spread around the entire world and had become the primary way of nourishing the bulk of the world's population. By then, the committed hunter-gatherers had become a minority and had been displaced to the margins of the civilized world. Just think about that for a second: This way of agricultural food production began only about 9000 to 10,000 years ago, and later than that in some places, and then by A.D. 1500—not terribly long ago in the time scale we're talking about—what had previously been the absolute total human approach to food gathering (that is, food procurement) was pushed to the margins and this new method, agricultural food production based on domesticates, had become by far the predominant method and it had spread around the world; only about a 7000-year period in order to accomplish that.

As I pointed out earlier, there are a number of locations of origin scattered around the world on several different continents. In a matter of this relatively short time, these isolated points of domestication had become centers for this new way of life, and then, of course, this style of producing food had to radiate out from these points and colonize the rest of the world. As we approach that subject, we have to keep in mind that this is a prehistoric issue, at least in the beginning; there are no written records, so in order to establish this story we have to approach it scientifically, we have to use a number of different methods. The first one that I want to talk about is the so-called biological method. This one is associated with a man named Vavilov who will appear later in this course, not so much because of this method but because of his role in the advancement of science and agriculture.

Vavilov, in the 1930s and 1940s, became deeply interested in this question: Where did agricultural lifestyles begin, and how did they move; where did domesticates go? In order to do that, he looked not at archaeological material, but he looked at living material. What he was really looking at, or trying to determine, was the amount of genetic diversity in any given plant species. For example, if you're talking about wheat, he would ask: How many different strains and types are there? How many different genetic varieties are there? Then he made an assumption: He thought if he could locate the actual center of genetic diversity—and when I say "center" I mean that Vavilov would map these locations; he would lay out a map of a region and then he would go out and take samples and he would note from where the samples came and he would look for genetic variety—and he made an assumption. His basic assumption was that where there was the most variety was likely to be the point of origin for that plant.

That may take a little thinking; why would that be? First of all, it would suggest that this is the place where there would have been the most trial and error, the most number of experiments, the number of things tried; it would have been closest probably to where the wild progenitors lived. It is also based on the concept that as these valuable plants—these domesticated plants—moved out, they didn't move out en masse. Samples were taken out that would be a small genetic portion—in genetics we sometimes call this a founder effect; just a small portion of the genetics were taken out—and then a new population started from that; so the genetic diversity in this separate place would be less. As you get farther and farther away from the point of origin, you get less and less genetic diversity. That's an interesting assumption; is it always correct? No, it's not; because we do know now that some plants were not necessarily domesticated at the places where their wild progenitors grew, and so on, so it's a good place to start.

If the wild progenitor in this case also is known, then looking at its geographical range and then adding this Vavilov approach of genetic variability really can focus you in quickly to the likely place where a particular origin may have occurred. This is really useful if you're talking about a creature with a narrow range. For example, sheep and goats: We know that the wild progenitors of sheep and goats had a natural range that was rather tight, rather small; and so we know using this genetic variability business and that range data you can really pretty well pinpoint where these things started. It's less useful when you have creatures with a very broad natural range. I'll give you as a couple examples bovines (cows) and pigs that really had wide ranges in nature long before any domestication events took place, and what that does, of course, is make the Vavilov method more difficult to use.

Another approach, and in a sense a more straightforward approach, is the archaeological approach. I assume that most of you have been thinking all along that this story we're telling is based on sort of archaeological artifacts, and it is to some extent, but not entirely; and that's the point of bringing these things up. The beginnings of the study of the origins of agriculture based on an archaeological approach can pretty much be attributed to an American, Robert Braidwood, who was associated with the University of Chicago's Oriental Institute. He started his work later than Vavilov, but the 2 actually did overlap in time; so there was some cross-fertilization, if I may use that word. Of course, Braidwood and his colleagues, and subsequently many others, had begun to look for archaeological material that would be useful in determining the story of how agriculture began, where it began, and ultimately how it moved.

Where did Braidwood start? He started in the Middle East, and using information that he could get from Vavilov-type studies, he didn't just start it random in the Middle East, he went to regions where there were accumulations of wild animals that were probably forebears of domesticates; so he was already hedging his bet and moving in that direction. What did he find? First of all, they looked in places like middens—garbage dumps—in these ancient excavations and they found things like bones, bone fragments, and teeth; they still found pottery, some of which had seeds and other plant material actually associated with it; and, of course, they found bone tools and stone tools and things of that sort, the kind of stuff you would expect to find in an archaeological dig.

What can you determine from things like that? I'm going to give you just one example to show you how these people put this kind of thing together. A good archaeologist with zoological training can often look at a bone or a bone fragment and determine one, its species; if he has the right bones, he can determine sex, usually pelvic bones and things; and if he has, again, the right material, he can sometimes determine age. If you have these 3 things—species, sex, and age—what can this tell you about domestication? If you're looking at a garbage dump, or a midden, put together by a group of hunter-gatherers who were simply out hunting these animals, what kind of bones are you likely to find with regard to species, age, and sex in this garbage dump? You'd find all the bones of a given species, let's say sheep; then you start looking at the age and you see a variety of ages; and you look at sex and you see a variety of sexes.

Then, relatively abruptly, as you get to newer material and you look in the garbage dump you suddenly see a very different distribution. Now you look at the bones of sheep and you discover that the bones you're finding are predominately male and predominately young. What does this tell you? A hunting culture is simply out killing the animals they can kill, dragging them back, slaughtering them, eating them, and throwing the bones away. But when suddenly you have just the bones of young males, you don't see many female bones and you don't see any young female bones, this suggests to you that you now have a managed flock; that this flock is being carefully managed, that these people have figured out that one male can impregnate a whole lot of females so they eat all the little males and keep all the females to increase the size of their flock. Clever analysis of this kind of archaeological material can give lots of insight into what was going on.

Some seeds can be identified as either wild type or domesticate, and that helps a great deal in figuring out when things began to be domesticated; and, of course, these people found tools and other kinds of artifacts, and these are very useful, but they have to be kept in context and they have to be looked at carefully. For example, there are some primitive tools that we look at and assume are agricultural and then might assume that the people that had them are these kinds of new agriculturalists (food producers). That wouldn't necessarily be the case, because some hunter-gatherers who did not domesticate plants and did not actually do farming did aid their efforts at harvesting by using some tools to go out and harvest wild plants and bring them back. So you have to be careful in analysis of tools; these things require that people become engaged and think carefully about them.

We can also begin to assign exact dates—how old something is—by using isotopic dating methods, and the most commonly used of those is carbon dating; and there's a reason for that. First of all, if you're interested in biological material, life on Earth is carbon-based; and so if you can date the carbon in a sample, you get an idea of how old it is, and if it's a biological sample it's going to have carbon in it. Carbon on Earth exists naturally in 2 isotopic forms. The principle one is C12; but there is also a radioactive unstable isotope C14. It's in very small percentage compared to C12; in fact, there's about a million million more times C12 than C14, about 10^{12} more C12 molecules than C14 molecules in the modern world. In a creature like myself, a modern creature, the distribution of C12 to C14 in my body should be something in the neighborhood of a million million times more C12 than C14.

But take an ancient sample: When the carbon is incorporated into that creature and that creature dies, then there's no carbon going in or carbon coming out. There's something special about C14: it decays, and it decays to C12. An old sample is going to have an even wider differential between C12 and C14, and since the half-life of C14 is well-established—it's 5730 years—we can look at the ratio of C14 to C12, and based on what that ratio is and knowing the half-life of C14 it is possible to extrapolate back from the present to when that sample laid down its carbon, when that creature was living. This is a very good technique for measuring the age of biological samples, and it's, of course, aided by the development of a wonderful instrument called the mass spectrometer that has the ability to separate atoms of things like carbon and then look at the different weights to tell a C14 isotope from a C12 isotope and in an automated fashion give you the number that you want and allow you to make the calculation that you want to make.

More recently, we now have molecular biology getting into the picture, and we have molecular biological techniques that also help us figure out where things originated and how they developed. Mitochondrial DNA work is based on knowing that mitochondria, the energy engine in an advanced cell, comes only from the mother in genetics; and, therefore, we can look at the DNA of this self-replicating molecule and follow matrilineally where creatures came from. We know now that the *Homo sapiens sapiens*, our species, came out of sub-Saharan Africa; most of the information for that comes from a combination of mitochondrial DNA work associated with Vavilov-type assumptions having to do with the amount of genetic diversity. Of course, now, with modern techniques using things like the polymerase chain reaction where we can greatly amplify a DNA sample and automatic sampling and sequencing techniques it's possible to really do a careful analysis of the sequence of a number of different DNA samples, again giving us very precise analysis of where certain things originated, and as we keep wanting to say in this lecture, where they're ultimately going to go.

Finally, archaeologists and linguists get together and do historical comparative linguistics, and this is a technique based on the assumption again that when language groups move it's because people move; the language isn't necessarily spread by other people picking it up, but native speakers tend to move into a region.

What you really have at the end of all this is a variety of approaches—archaeology, biology, molecular biology, physics, and linguistics—all asking the same question, and when you start to get agreement among these different approaches then your confidence grows because the evidence supports itself. That's how these stories have been developed: there weren't any eyewitnesses left, we don't have written records, but we have got careful science and it's coming from various sources and it's being put together to tell the story.

What about the spread of agriculture? There certainly are several models about how agriculture moved from individual points of origin to different places around the globe. We think—in fact, we're pretty sure, using these methods—that agriculture moved by diffusing into new areas; but that means only that we think it wasn't started de novo in a number of different places, sort of in a continuum, but rather it spread from places of origin into new regions, but we don't know exactly how that could happen. I could give you 2 examples immediately for how agriculture could diffuse into a new area: One, people could emulate it; they could either be impressed by it and take it up themselves, or it could be imposed on them by someone taking them over and saying, "You plow this field and you do it and you can eat some of the stuff," or pioneers can move into an area bringing their agricultural techniques with them. In many cases, we probably had both things happening; but both of these models suggest that agriculture spread out from points of origin and just didn't pop up de novo and ultimately cover most of the globe.

Agriculturalists, then—people who were committed to this lifeway of producing their own food—often found themselves associated with neighboring hunter-gather types (food procurers), and there's evidence that these people often lived side-by-side, sometimes for extended periods of time; it could go on for hundreds of years. What do we know about these relationships of these people with each other? We know that some agricultural settlements were fortified. That tells us something; it tells us that the people who lived there were concerned enough about their security that they fortified their settlement. But we don't know who they were concerned with; were they concerned with their neighboring hunter-gatherers, or were they concerned with other agriculturalists that might be living nearby? This is an interesting issue that isn't always easy to sort out.

We also know that because there were different kinds of hunter-gatherers in these regions and different kinds of potential domesticates, when agriculturalists moved in, in very different places they found different kinds of situations. That means that it's very difficult to develop a sweeping model for how agriculture spread from points of origin to where it finally ended up. It was probably different in each locale because you had different indigenous people living there, you had different interactions between the 2, and you had different results in each place. However, again, we keep trying to look for overreaching theoretical pictures.

One, I talk about the diffusion of agriculture as opposed to de novo starting; there seems to be another sort of uniform situation, and that is when hunter-gatherers, when food procurers, themselves do adopt agricultural ways of life, there seem to be similar ways that they do this. In the first place, they have to have availability; they have to know about the advantages of domesticated animals and domesticated plants. They have to see them, they have to know about the advantages of them, and then they have to get into the issue of substitution. They have to get these materials—we think they probably got them often through trade, but, of course, we know there's another way you could get these things: you could steal them—but they have to be able to get these things and then substitute them for the wild sources of food that they had previously been using. The last step appears to be what's called consolidation, and that is the weaving of this food-production approach into the cultural background that these people already have. You can see that in a number of different places there are going to be a number of different ways that agriculture actually took root.

We know that there were a number of sites for the start or origin of agriculture, and there are really 7 of them that have been particularly well-studied; we know there are more than that, but there are 7 that get a lot of attention. It was long felt that the earliest domestication events and agricultural practices occurred in the Fertile Crescent. But again, this is science; and even now we should know that there are claims suggesting that maybe there are older places of origin. The other regions beyond the Fertile Crescent included Mexico, South China, North China, the Central Andes, the Eastern United States, and even sub-Saharan Africa. We know that from the Fertile Crescent, agricultural practices moved first into Anatolia—which, of course, is part of modern Turkey—and then across into Mediterranean Europe and southern Europe. Agriculture then traveled up the Danube—which you may recall goes, of course, north from that area and also turns west—and that took agriculture into essentially temperate Europe. We know that by 6000 years ago before the present agriculture did exist in the British Isles; so it got that far.

We also know that agriculture spread eastward from Southwest Asia into eastern Europe, and that went all the way to the Eurasian steppes in what is really modern Hungary, where it sort of stopped going in that direction for about 600 years. Agriculture also radiated out from points of origin in East Asia and Southeast Asia into Oceania. The people who often colonized the islands of Oceania were probably familiar with agriculture before they went there. The Indian Subcontinent is the site of some initial domestications—we know that, and when we talk about specific domestications we'll talk about India—but we also know that agriculture in India blended with agriculture coming from the east, and also later with agriculture that came around from the west and the north.

Though agriculture appears to have spread from Southeast Asia into North Africa fairly early, sub-Saharan Africa may have been an independent focus for the early development of agriculture in the Neolithic period; remember, that's where our species originated, but it's not a place where we think we started agriculture first. Agriculture also appears to have radiated out from several independent centers in the Americas. One such location was in what is now the Southeastern United States; the Andes and parts of Mesoamerica were also areas that developed their own forms of agriculture.

As I pointed out before, the specific patterns for the origins of agriculture were different in these different places for a number of the reasons that I mentioned. It is clear that the transformation to food production was not accomplished in the same way from place to place. There is evidence for food producers and food procurers living in close proximity to each other and affecting each other in different ways and providing different patterns. The patterns followed depended, again, upon the resources available, the regional practices of the people who were already there, and the conditions that allowed for food production. In the Fertile Crescent, there were examples of integrated farmers fairly early in the development of agriculture. What do we mean by integrated farmers? We mean people who were horticulturists; they essentially raised plants. But they also integrated that with what we call pastoral forms of agriculture: They herded and maintained animals. They were integrated; that's one kind of farming.

We also know that there are people who are dedicated pastoralists; that they really don't do much crop farming, but they tend flocks or herds. We also know that there are people who are pretty much dedicated horticulturists who live primarily by the plants they can grow and don't really integrate that with animal agriculture. But we see all kinds of sort of hybrid situations, again, depending on the circumstances. We know that, for example, some dedicated pastoralists do supplement their diets by foraging as they go along with their animals, and they do some hunting and some fishing. We know that dedicated horticulturists—people who plant and tend plants—also supplement their diets with hunting and so on. That's clearly important to people who live right around me: My agricultural neighbors keep their freezers full by hunting; hunting is an important aspect of balancing their diet.

To demonstrate how site specific some of these patters were, it's known that some dedicated agriculturists reverted to hunting and gathering if the circumstances were conducive to that. We know that the people who went to Oceania knew about agriculture, they were agriculturalists; but they sometimes found islands that were uninhabited by other people and that were rich in flora and fauna.

These people often gave up their agricultural ways and adopted hunting-gathering lifestyles until their population density and their impact on the native flora and fauna forced them back. But it shows again that the lifestyle of hunter-gatherers can be essentially more attractive sometimes than the hard work of farming.

Despite evidence that farmers and gathers can live in close proximity, it's undeniable that the food producing way of life did come to dominate. By A.D. 1500, the vast majority of the people on Earth were sustained by food that was produced by agriculture. By then, the hunting-gathering people, as I pointed out before, were excluded to the margins of the civilized world. That will take us, then, to a point where we can start in the next lecture talking about the impact of the way that agriculture and the dependence on agricultural food production impacted the physical and biological environment, and how some of the problems that modern men are facing as we look at the impacts of agriculture began with our prehistoric origins.

Thank you.

Lecture Five
Agriculture Impacts Ecology and Geology

Scope:

Estimates suggest that Earth's population was between 1 and 5 million at the beginning of the Neolithic period. By the year 1350, it had grown to as many as 300 million. More mouths to feed meant that land must be used more intensely and that more of it must be under production. This 2-pronged effort has had a significant impact on ecosystems. As the present population of Earth struggles with the challenges of population growth and environmental preservation, we would do well to realize that the roots of these problems lie in our prehistoric past.

Outline

I. In this lecture, we begin an examination of the impacts agricultural practices have on the environment.

II. We first discuss the nexus between food production and population size. This is part of the carrying capacity consideration.

    A. The carrying capacity of an environment is a balance between an organism's biotic potential and environmental pressure. Exceeding the carrying capacity can have catastrophic consequences for the organism involved; this is why environmentalists concern themselves with tipping points and points of no return.

    B. Homeostasis in biological systems is the result of self-regulating negative feedback loops. Positive feedback, on the other hand, is not self-regulating but autocatalytic.

    C. The food production–population nexus constitutes a positive feedback for food producers. However, it is not necessarily a positive feedback for food procurers. That suggests that this nexus will not lead to stasis but rather to fundamental change in the system.

    D. How sustainable is the ongoing growth in the human population? What is Earth's present carrying capacity for human beings? Though there is no shortage of persons willing to offer answers to these questions, my own impression is that at this time, nobody really knows.

III. As stated before, there are only 2 options for increasing agricultural output. You can use the land more efficiently and more intensely, or you can use more of it.

IV. By definition, agriculture begins to exert a level of control over nature that is human generated. The more intensely we employ agriculture and the more of it we do, the greater our impact on the physical and biological components of our environment.

V. Another example of the way domestication affected Earth's land form and ecology is the way in which early farmers cleared land: They often cut down or burned forests and groves of trees.

VI. Irrigation is used in many places to increase production on land that is dry or has unpredictable rainfall. Irrigation methods, too, have had an impact on Earth's geology and ecology.

  A. Irrigation is essential in many parts of the world to produce crops and in other locals is employed to attain optimum cropping conditions.

  B. There are a number of different types of irrigation, some more sustainable than others.

  C. River flooding of the kind that occurs in the Nile basin can be self-sustaining and go on almost indefinitely.

  D. Other types of irrigation can result in silting and salinization, which can eventually make land unfit for crop production.

Suggested Reading:

Hillel, *Out of the Earth*, chaps. 11–15.

Sweeney, *Agriculture in the Middle Ages*, chap. 5.

Questions to Consider:

1. Can you think of some modern examples of agricultural impacts on ecology and geology?

2. Soils require a variety of nutrients to remain productive in agriculture. What are a few basic ways that people have attempted to maintain or improve the nutrient content of soil?

3. Can you give examples of the collapse or demise of civilizations or societies as a result of their agricultural practices?

Lecture Five—Transcript
Agriculture Impacts Ecology and Geology

In the last lecture, we discussed the effect of the beginnings of plant and animal domestication on modern humans, *Homo sapiens sapiens*, and the early settled communities that those humans were establishing. That brings us to this discussion of the impact that domestication was having upon the Earth, the changes that domestication brought to ecology and the geology in the areas where human beings were evolving from food procurers to food producers.

Some estimates suggest that the population of the world was between 1 and 5 million at the beginning of the Neolithic period that we are discussing, about 10,000 years before the present. That has grown to 150 million by the beginning of the 1st century. By 1350, there were as many as 300 million humans on the Earth. As we pointed out, more mouths to feed meant land must be used more intensely or more of it must be used. As agricultural food production became the norm and the population began to expand, our species had little choice but to follow both approaches, and that meant to put more land under production and to use that land more intensely. This 2-pronged effort to exert more control over nature has had, and continues to have, significant impact on surrounding environs and also on global systems. As the present population of Earth struggles with the balancing act that must occur between producing sufficient nourishment for an ever-increasing number of people and preserving the environment which has allowed our species unprecedented success since the end of the last mega climate change, we would do well to realize that the roots of these problems lie in our ancient, prehistoric past.

In the previous lecture, we discussed the emergence of agriculture as the primary way of feeding people and its spread around much of the globe. In this lecture, we will begin an examination of the impacts agricultural practices have on the environment. In order to begin this discussion, we'll need a brief discussion of the food production-population size nexus. In other words, what I'm talking about here as a nexus is that relationship between the size of the population and how much food needs to be produced to take care of that population; the larger the population, obviously, the more food that has to be produced. In biology, we would say that this is part of the carrying

©2009 The Teaching Company.

capacity consideration. Carry capacity for us will be an extremely important concept.

The carrying capacity of an environment is a balance between an organism's biotic potential—that is, its ability to reproduce itself—and the environmental pressure. Exceeding the carrying capacity can have catastrophic consequences for an organism involved. Let me take a few minutes and explain that carrying capacity situation a little more thoroughly and then give you an example. Biotic potential is the built-in potential of an organism to reproduce. Human beings have significant biotic potential. Ours is not as significant as, for example, some insects that can make billions of offspring in a very short time; it takes us a little longer to do it, but our survival rates give us good biotic potential. That pushes up the number of individuals. Environmental resistance is what's pushing down on biotic potential. It's things like lack of food, lack of space, inappropriate places or lack of appropriate places for mating, and so on, overcrowding, wastes; all that sort of stuff pushes down on the population numbers. So there's this tension, the potential to produce more individuals, and the potential to push them down; and that reaches a balance point called the carrying capacity, which is a description for what is sort of a constant maximum regulatable level for organisms in a given environment. That's the carrying capacity; and it looked like from those numbers we gave you before that when human beings were living as hunter-gatherers—before we became food producers—we had a carrying capacity for a few million people on planet Earth; that was the sort of balanced situation where the carrying capacity could keep things under control.

But if you exceed the carrying capacity, things can go wrong. Let's use an example of a situation that really took place: An island in a lake in the north was devoid of large animal inhabitants—there were no deer, elk, or moose on that particular island—hence it had abundance of food for such creatures. At some point, a breeding pair—a male and a female—of these elk were deposited on that island. There were no predators and they had abundant food, so what did they do? They ate, they grew, they got busy, and they established a family. They started to have little elk, and the little elk interbred, and soon the population really began to grow, and you can see the population numbers go up, up, up, up, up. Then, of course, what happens? Food starts to become limiting. If the carrying capacity has not been exceeded, when food becomes limiting, that's environmental pressure and the population drops a little bit and then the food recovers and the population goes back up because of its biotic potential. But if you exceed the carrying capacity, something different happens, and it happened in this instance. There got to be so many elk on that island that they began to eat not just the under forest, but they began to nibble off all the branches and they took the forest floor down to practically nothing.

What happens? They had to wait through the winter for more material to grow back up, but they couldn't; animals don't store food for long periods of time, they can't can or freeze. So what happened? All of them died; the population didn't just drop back down, their success at breeding overwhelmed the capacity of the carrying capacity to regulate things. They consumed more than could be replaced in a reasonable period of time and the end result is catastrophic: The population didn't decline, it crashed to zero. It is for reasons like this that environmentalists often concern themselves with things like tipping points and points of no return, because that's what happened to those elk on that island.

Homeostasis in biological systems is the result of self-regulating negative feedback loops; that's pretty common stuff in biology: Your body temperature stays constant because of a series of negative feedback loops; they work in all sorts of ways to maintain constant conditions. Positive feedback, on the other hand, is not self-regulating but is autocatalytic. It means it catalyzes more of itself; the more you have, the more you're going to make. We introduced this point earlier using labor pains as an example of positive feedback and a thermostat as an example of negative feedback.

The food production-population nexus that I just mentioned constitutes a positive feedback for food producers; not for hunter-gatherers, not for creatures that are simply living in nature taking from the environment what it has, but you change everything when you put control over nature and begin to produce food, you change that food production-population nexus. Note it is not necessarily a positive feedback for food procurers. That suggests that it is our food-population nexus which will not lead to stasis, but rather to a fundamental change in the system. Let me say that one more time so that we're very clear on what I'm saying: It is that food-population nexus that is a positive feedback loop that's not going to lead to a stasis, but rather we're afraid that it's going to lead to some kind of fundamental change in the system. If that change comes as a result of exceeding the carrying capacity, that's not going to be a pleasant time in which to be around.

The foregoing points beg the question: How sustainable is the ongoing growth in the human population, and what is the present carrying capacity of the Earth for human beings (some big questions)? Though there is no shortage of persons willing to offer answers to those questions, my own impression is that at this time, nobody really knows. We're going to return to that subject in the final lectures of this course.

As I stated before, there are only 2 options for increasing agricultural output: You can use the land more effectively and more intensely, or you can use more of it. By definition, agriculture begins to exert a level of control over nature that is human-generated. The more intensely we employ agriculture and the more of it we do the greater our impact on the physical and biological components of our environment; that's just inescapable. Let's discuss the effect of some specific cases: the different effects of those who manage animal herds, and those who cultivate domesticated plants.

Pastoralists alter the balance between predators and prey. Most of the creatures that pastoralists tend are prey for some kind of wild predator; we know from our fairy tales as children that wolves eat sheep, and if you are a pastoralist that is herding sheep, what is your response to wolves? You're going to try to take them out of the environment. Hunting wolves, killing wolves, driving wolves away is not a frowned upon activity among early pastoralists herding sheep. In so doing, then, they also change the carrying capacity for their domesticates. If the predators are part of the environmental pressure, part of the environmental resistance, pushing down on your lamb flock keeping the numbers constant and you take away the predators, you've changed the carrying capacity; you've now allowed for more sheep to live in this area. When you do that, what happens? When you change the carrying capacity for your domesticates, that, in turn, changes the predator-prey balance between grazing domesticates and their forage. You may be a little puzzled by that terminology: You may not think of a sheep eating grass as a predator eating prey, but, in fact, that's what it is; it's eating essentially its prey, and you changed the balance now because you took the wolves out of the picture and you had more sheep. The sheep are now putting more pressure on the forage. That can, and has led, to widespread soil erosion that affects the fertility of the soil and the quality of surface water and the air.

Let me give you an example: Early agricultural practice in Greece had that effect. The first farmers in Greece were agropastoralists that had emigrated from Anatolia (Turkey). They found a land sparsely inhabited by food procurers and their settlements rapidly grew in number and they spread quickly into new, hospitable regions. They had sheep, goats, and pigs which they tended, as well as the ability to grow crops of wheat, barley, and lentils. These folks were pretty well-established, integrated farmers; animal farming, plant farming. These colonizing pioneers began arriving around 8000 years ago; between 1000 and 500 years after their arrival the signs of agricultural environmental damage were extremely evident. Just in that short period of time, massive soil erosion brought on by overgrazing and poor cultivation techniques stripped the soil from the hills that were the sites of these first agricultural colonies. What was left behind was bare rock, altering the landscape to this day. When we think of that Greek landscape, that's often what we think of; it didn't look like that before these people came there, essentially—and I'll use the word—unwittingly or unknowingly used the land, and destroyed it. Incidentally, there was a rapid and significant decline in the population of those peoples (not surprising).

Another example of the way domestication affected Earth's land form and ecology is the way in which farmers cleared land. In order to obtain more tillable land, early farmers often cut down or burned forests and groves of trees in order to obtain more land to be used for crops or for grazing of their domesticated animals. Often the wood from those trees was put to very good use as building material or as fuel for shelter, tools, farming implements, and, of course, sometimes for weapons; that seems to be sort of the nature of our species. It should be noted that humans have had a long and productive association with trees. Over the millennia, a number of fruit and nut trees were domesticated as well as a fair number of trees that could be used for specialized building purposes such as sailing ships and special dwelling places; so again, domesticates were also opening up trade and communication. Those of us with "bookish" tendencies have a special warm spot for woody plants that provide pulp to be used for paper. By the way, paper is said to have been invented around A.D. 105 in China.

©2009 The Teaching Company.

Many trees were of great import to man throughout the past 10,000 years without ever being actually domesticated, even though some were cultivated in a kind of systematic Sylva culture or forest culture. We talk about a "sylvan glade," that's a forest glad; Sylva culture is a kind of agriculture for trees, and it was possible to bring some trees under cultivation, if you will—plant them and look after them—but not really necessarily fit our definition for domestication because those trees probably are not either phenotypically or genetically different from a wild progenitor.

Slash and burn techniques, an alternate way of clearing land to chopping trees down, quickly produced more useable land, but little of value was actually recoverable from the trees that once occupied the land. Tree roots and the roots of the forest understory are essential in maintaining topsoil in many environments. When the trees were removed and the network of roots disturbed, soil erosion on a large scale can and often did take place. Since trees conduct photosynthesis on a very large scale, the loss of significant numbers of trees reduces the availability of oxygen in the atmosphere, but of even greater consequence may be that more carbon dioxide is left in the atmosphere; and you know that CO_2 is one of those greenhouse gases.

I passed rather quickly over photosynthesis, oxygen, and CO_2; let's take just a moment to review what many of you I'm sure know about photosynthesis, but let's be sure. Photosynthesis is a light-driven process. Its purpose seems to be to take the most oxidized form of carbon that exists in the atmosphere, CO_2, and reduce it to the level of cell material, or down to the level of a sugar. So the net reaction is to take CO_2, and, using light as the driving force, put electrons and essentially hydrogen ions on that CO_2, hook the CO_2s together, and make them into sugar. Where do the hydrogen ions come from? In green plant photosynthesis, those hydrogen ions come from water. Photosynthesis splits water, uses the hydrogen ions and the electrons, attaches them to CO_2 and takes it out of the atmosphere; and by splitting the water, it releases oxygen which goes up into the atmosphere. Photosynthesis is doing just the opposite of respiration with regard to CO_2 and oxygen; and that's why it's very important to maintain an appropriate balance between photosynthetic plants and respiring animals, or the activities of respiring animals on planet Earth, so as not to upset that balance.

Irrigation is employed in many places in order to increase production on land that is dry or has unpredictable rainfall. Irrigation methods, too, have had an impact upon the Earth's geology and ecology. Irrigation is essential in many parts of the world to produce crops, and in other locales it's employed to attain optimum cropping conditions. There are a number of different types of irrigation; some are more sustainable than others. We have the situation in the Tigris-Euphrates Valley where we know that settlers came in to the lower end of the valley and began a kind of irrigation that caused salination in the land around where the irrigation was taking place. One, this reduced the productivity and those people moved up the rivers and exerted their authority on others to find better places to farm; but also, it's interesting to note what happened in terms of the plants, because when these people began their irrigation they were planting wheat. But wheat is fairly sensitive to salt, and the wheat began to have real difficulties growing. The people who came in behind them planted barley, which is much more salt-tolerant. You can see that sort of salination wave and a movement of barley up the Tigris-Euphrates. River flooding of the kind that occurs in the Nile basin can be self-sustaining and can go on almost indefinitely, as, in fact, it has. Other types of irrigation can result in silting and salination which can eventually make land unfit for crop production.

In the concluding lectures of this course, we will be examining the current global food-production system. As we approach that subject, it will be important to understand that agriculture, from its earliest beginnings, has had significant and increasing impacts on the environment. There were undoubtedly mistakes made as humans learned to employ their new agricultural techniques. Look at the examples we used here today: the situation with those first agro people who moved into Greece and essentially ruined their own program by causing massive soil erosion and essentially leaving the land in a condition that we can see today, thousands of years later. For well over 100 millennia prior to the Neolithic Revolution, human population numbers had been reasonably constant, as we pointed out before, maintained by the carrying capacity of the environment for a creature such as ourselves. With the advent of agriculture and the accompanying efforts to exert ever more control over the natural world, early agriculturists began to alter the carrying capacity and as a consequence expand their numbers.

The human domestication of plants and animals and the agricultural enterprise, from a very early time, has had significant impact on the land, surface, and subsurface water and on the air. The practice of agriculture which sustains us and supports our enormously expanded population continues to have profound impacts on our environment, which in turn greatly affect the non-domesticated plants and animals living around us. Just to point that out, let me give one more example there, not far from where a number of you may live: what's happening in the Chesapeake Bay. The Chesapeake Bay was the richest estuary in the world at one time. It was spilling over with shellfish and crabs, and it was a very easy place to get seafood. As agriculture began to become more intense upstream, up the Susquehanna River which empties down into the Chesapeake Bay, what happened? Silt from agriculture, runoff from manure, and runoff from fertilizers began to get into all the tributaries of the Susquehanna and into the Susquehanna itself, and it began to flow down into the Chesapeake. We began to note a number of years ago that there was a region that was simply called the "dead zone"; that's pretty dramatic, isn't it? It's a part of the Chesapeake where things no longer grow; things that we're interested in like shellfish, clams, oysters, and things of that sort. They're gone; it's a dead zone.

People began to look very carefully at what was going on. I'm sorry to have to report that year by year that dead zone seems to get bigger, despite our efforts to ameliorate the problem. The problem is manifold; it is true—there is urban sewage waste getting into the water and whatnot—but let's face it: A very significant component of the pollution getting into the Susquehanna and ending up in the Chesapeake creating this huge dead zone is from agricultural practice. We need the agriculture; we need to feed people, we need to use the land more intensely. That means fertilizers, that means stocking rates of cattle; but there are prices to pay, and it's being paid right now, for example, in the Chesapeake Bay.

It is important to be aware that the roots of these modern problems lie in our ancient, prehistoric past because it gives us a more nuanced and informed approach to the current discussions and debates about how best to resolve the struggle between competing interests relating to land use, food production, and protection of the environment.

Lecture Six
You Are What You Eat, Raise, and Build

Scope:

From about 10,000 to 5000 years before the present, there arose a rich tapestry of different peoples cooperating, competing, fighting, and cohabiting. This variety in people had a great deal to do with the plants and animals that they were domesticating and tending. Just as animals and plants met humans partway, so did humans adapt over time to the behaviors and needs of their domesticates. We discuss the earliest trajectory of this change and how tending crops and herds of animals helped form the collective character of civilization and the roots of our basic attitudes toward such things as time, work, leisure, and distance.

Outline

I. Just as domestication has had an impact on plants and animals, so, too, has the interaction changed humans.

II. Different kinds of agriculturally based societies probably arose due to several factors—climate change, increased population, and possible overhunting of larger animals.

III. There are some interesting differences between the 2 types of communities that developed.

    A. Pastoralists were animal tenders. This involved the development and management of a herd of animals that provided people with meat or skin, wool, hair, milk, manure, transport, and even housing.

        1. Hunter-gatherers hunted whatever animals were available. Pastoralists, on the other hand, grew to depend on the specific animal they raised and managed.

        2. While hunter-gatherers moved at will to follow a variety of species of game, pastoralists moved in accord with the needs of just a few types of animals upon which they depended.

        3. Pastoralists were watchful for predators and assumed the alpha role in the flock or herd, leading the animals to food, water, shelter, and safety.

        4. Pastoralists learned to be surgeon, midwife, drill sergeant, and even animal psychologist.

B. Horticulturists were crop farmers. *Horto* is Latin for "garden."

   1. Horticulturalist communities tended to stay near available water sources, while pastoralists tended to come from more arid places.

   2. Horticulturists developed axes and adzes to clear the land and hoes and digging sticks to cultivate it.

C. The physical environment has a significant impact on the development of who we are; in combination with a given domesticate, it can be the most important factor in shaping a culture.

D. There were real differences in the kinds of work and time commitments required for tending crops versus herding animals.

E. Issues of territoriality were also affected by the type of food-producing activity being engaged in.

IV. It was rather natural that the evolution to a community of people who both raised crops and tended animals occurred. We can still see this division among modern people: those who are primarily pastoralists, those who are primarily horticulturalists, and those who do both (the mixed farmer).

A. There are differences in the way each organizes schedules, depending on the needs of their crops or herds.

   1. Horticulturists who depend primarily on cereal grains are intensely busy during planting and harvest.

   2. Pastoralists can have similarly characteristic approaches to time management and scheduling, depending on the animals they are tending.

B. Differences in the physiology of the animals also have implications for our discussion here. Sheep, goats, and bovines are ruminants with multiple stomachs. That means they can digest cellulose and tolerate more difficult grazing areas than, for example, horses.

V. Even the kinds of gods worshiped were often affected by the domesticates with which people partnered.

Suggested Reading:

There is no suggested reading for this lecture.

Questions to Consider:

1. Try to give biological reasons for why Genghis Khan invaded peoples to his west and was successful in his conquests.

2. The cuisine of Europe can be divided among those countries that are olive oil based and those that are butter based (with the exception of France, of course, where both are liberally used). What is the reason for this, and what effects does it likely have on culture?

3. Western movies are replete with tales of conflict between sheep herders and cattlemen. What stereotypes are affixed to each group? Why do you think the ruminate being husbanded would have such a profound effect on culture?

Lecture Six—Transcript
You Are What You Eat, Raise, and Build

Hello; and welcome back. In the course thus far, we have seen that the conversion to agriculture made enormous differences in the lives of our domesticated plants and animals, the ecology of the environment and the actual climate of the Earth, but it also began to make significant changes in us. From about 10,000 to 5000 years before the present, there arose a rich tapestry of different peoples cooperating, competing, fighting, and cohabitating. There grew up trade, coercion, cooperation, exchange of ideas; obviously a rich and vigorous variety. This variety in people had, and has, a great deal to do with the plants and animals that people were domesticating and tending. We've mentioned before that domestication is a 2-way street rather than a unilateral imposition of will. Just as the animals and plants met humans part way, so did humans adapt over time to the behaviors and needs of the domesticates they tended and were becoming increasingly dependent upon. These adaptations differed; they differed depending upon what you raised, what you ate, what you built upon, and what your own prior experiences were.

Herding animals shaped human culture and interaction, and cultivating plants shaped civilization. The fact is that domesticating plants and animals changed *Homo sapiens sapiens* as much as they changed the domesticates, and we'll discuss the earliest trajectory of that change and how tending crops and herds of animals helped form the "collective character" of civilization and the roots of our basic attitudes toward such fundamental things as time, work, leisure, distance, responsibility, and commitment; these things were tied to those early cultures and the needs often brought on by the domesticates.

I'd like to start with an example from Hollywood, because it helps me introduce this idea that just as domestication has had an impact upon plants and animals, so, too, has it changed the humans in this interaction. Anyone familiar with the genre of the Western movie knows that there were supposedly significant differences between the outlooks, attitudes, and behaviors of stereotypical "cattlemen" and "sheep herders." The tensions between these 2 groups were thought to reside in the grazing habits of the 2 species of herbivores being husbanded, because sheep graze close to the ground damaging the forage for cattle in sparse environments. It's not a problem if the pastures are lush, but the Western movies were always shown out on the open rage where the sagebrush was far apart. In that situation, the sheep may have created a problem for the cattle. The movies frequently played on the assumed aggression and bellicosity of the mounted cattlemen and the predictable docility of the sheep tenders. I think these moviemakers were actually on to something, and by the end of the lecture, I hope you'll see what I mean.

Different kinds of agriculturally-based societies probably arose due to several factors. We know that climate change may have kicked things off, that increased population played a role, and that there needed to be more food made available in order to feed these growing populations. Each one of these societies and each one of these places where agriculture was beginning faced a special set of challenges and opportunities based on environment and the needs of the domesticates upon which it was depending; and I think also, as I mentioned before, some of the previous outlooks that their tribe or their group brought with them into that situation. I think culture was already beginning to play some role here.

It seems that there was one, big, single divergence in the type of early settlements of our hunting-gatherer forebears. Some communities evolved into pastoralists or animal tenders and some communities evolved more into horticulturalists or crop farmers. Whether a community tended animals or raised crops had to do, in large part, with their proximity to water. In order to water animals, pastoralists could drive them to a water source. They could then, and did, often settle in more arid parts of the world. Horticulturalists, on the other hand, had to live nearer the water sources. Water is heavy and difficult to transport long distances, so you find horticultural excursions into arable regions, ones that are inherently farmable. By the mid-Neolithic period, we find evidence of this transitional stage in the evolution of civilization: nomadic communities that were primarily pastoralists but were already beginning to take an advanced view toward managing the animals they were moving, and those that were primarily horticulturists, beginning to domesticate their plants.

There were some interesting differences between the 2 types of communities. Pastoralists, in this situation: This involved the development and management of a herd of animals that provided the people with meat or skin to be used as leather, wool, hair, milk, manure which was a very good fuel for some of these people, transport, and even housing in the form of tent coverings. Hunter-

©2009 The Teaching Company.

gatherers hunted any number of animals depending upon what was available. Pastoralists, on the other hand, grew to depend upon the specific animal that they raised and managed. So while hunter-gatherers moved at will to follow a variety of species of game, pastoralists moved in accord with the needs of the single type or at best a few the few types of animals upon which they were depending.

This didn't happen all at once, of course, but it evolved over time and over generations. As pastoralists learned to better care for their animals and managed their reproduction, the herd or flock grew and flourished. As the herd grew, there was more food available and the population of the people also increased. As that population increased, the health and well-being of the animals grew more critical because the contribution of the animals had to keep up with the growing demand of an expanding population. You can see how this probably happened: There was a shift from hunting and gathering whatever could be found or caught in the deliberate raising of a particular kind of creature. Eventually, movement or settlement of human beings was as much for the well-being of the animals as it was for the humans. This was a radical change from the way the hunter-gatherer chose to move or settle.

Pastoralists needed to be attentive and watchful for predators and had to assume, if you will, the alpha role in the flock or herd leading the animals to food, water, shelter, and safety. They needed to learn to be surgeon, midwife, drill sergeant, and even animal psychologists. Domestic animals often become dependent on people to help them with, for example, things like birthing; and this is interesting, this shows again this interplay between people and their domesticates. Because human beings often intervened in difficult births, attempting to save both the mother and the offspring—because they were both, if you will, important economic units; they wanted these animals, the animals were important, so they made a major effort to save the mother and offspring—who would likely have perished in the wild setting, but people intervene and save them; thus an environmental pressure based upon birthing difficulties was simply removed and these creatures and their genetics survived in the flock or herd, making that flock or herd progressively more dependant upon the shepherd or herdsman.

I'm intensely aware of this, because I raise sheep, and sheep have been under domestication for about 9000 years. Shepherds have been saving ewes and lambs carefully for a long time, and domestic sheep do have fairly frequent birthing problems. What is one way to resolve that problem? It may seem hardhearted, but one of the ways to do it is to say, "I'm going to stop intervening in these situations, and I'm going to let nature take its course." If you do that, difficult as it may be financially and emotionally to watch it, you will, in fact, by culling these genes out of your flock improve the birthing capacities of the whole flock. But that was certainly not being done much by our early pastoralist ancestors because they really needed those animals because their population was growing.

Horticulturalists: The "Horto," of course, is Latin for "garden." As we noted before, horticulturalist communities tended to stay near available water sources while pastoralists tended to come from the more arid places; animals can be driven to their water source; water must be hauled to crops. We've discussed the changes in some plants that domestication brought about: thinner or thicker seed coats, for example, or a rachis that held onto seeds rather than dispersing them. But there were changes to the human beings who cultivated food and who came to depend upon their food to sustain their growing population. Responding to the specific needs of the crops, these humans developed axes and adzes to clear the land and hoes and digging sticks to cultivate it. Those tools were developed by horticulturalists in order to more effectively till the land and improve the crop yield. Tools were developed by pastoralists to do other things: to slaughter animals and to prepare the meat, as well as to scrape and sew hides.

The type of domesticate and the terrain and climate had a major impact on the way land was viewed, shared, valued, and taken care of. Pastoralists tend to roam over a broad landscape returning regularly with their beasts to a fixed settlement, while horticulturists tend to live close to their fields, cover less ground, and choose landscapes that are not too hilly, rocky, wet, or dry; in other words, they're looking for good farmland. The physical environment has its own significant impact upon the development of who we are and the physical environment in combination with a given domesticate can be the most important factors in shaping an early emerging culture. For example, if it were not for the sled dog, the Inuit could not have successfully entered their harsh environment. But once that was done, however, they developed a distinctive and unique culture in order to cope with the challenges and best employ their assets. If it weren't for those dogs, you wouldn't be seeing these cultural adaptations of the Inuit to this very special environment to which thcy went.

Researchers suggest that the camel's water conserving abilities and ability to survive on sparse and poor quality vegetation in the Near East permitted their pastoralist herders to explore areas they did not have access to on foot as hunter-gatherers. There were real differences in the kinds of work and time commitments required in tending crops and herding animals. Horticulturists found themselves often tied to the seasons and the weather. Depending upon the crop being grown, they might experience periods of intense labor interspersed with periods of relative leisure. Issues of territoriality were also affected by the type of food producing activity being engaged in.

As populations grew, the pastoralist and horticulturist communities became less mobile because of the effort it took to raise sufficient food. In the latter years of the Neolithic period, we find evidence that communities consisted more and more of mixed or integrated farming: Individuals who had raised animals in a more or less nomadic, roaming way, began to settle in one spot and to cultivate crops as well. The combining of the technologies of horticulture with animal husbandry emerged in the later years of the Neolithic era and paved the way to intensified agriculture and the rise of civilization.

The increased size of the animal herds began to require a steady supply of—guess what—cultivated food. Let's pause for a second and think about what that just said. For a long time, pastoralists just moved their animals around and the animals ate from the land; the animals were essentially hunting and gathering and the pastoralists were managing them, while the horticulturalists were growing crops and feeding their families and themselves. But now when you begin to bring the animals into a fixed place and you keep them close to you so you can manage the flock or the herd and you can assist with the birthing, the animals are quickly going to eat the available food right down to the ground. What do you do? You essentially put your arms around them, if you will, and in a sense bring them into your family. You start cultivating food not only for yourself but for them, too. Now that's in a sense cultivating food for yourself because you're going to ultimately eat these animals, take their milk, or something; but when we started to feed our animals, that extended things a step beyond just letting them roam and graze.

Horticulturalists who were more involved with the cultivation of larger fields no doubt welcomed the domestic animals as a much more easily-acquired source of meat products than the wild game that they had to depend on before. So it was rather natural with this evolution to a community of people who both raised crops and tended animals took place. The mixed or integrated farmer could utilize a broader range of environments than either the pastoralists or the horticulturalists in some ways, but had to make technological and social adjustments to maintain animals closer to the settlement and to the crops.

It strikes me that we still can see this division between the modern person making a living primarily as a pastoralist and the modern person making a living primarily as a horticulturalist, and those who do both: the mixed farmer or integrated farmer. There are differences in the way each will organize and manage time and schedules, depending upon the needs of their crops or herds, for example. Horticulturists who depend primarily on cereal grains are intensely busy during planting and harvest. Their grain seeds can be stored effectively, however, so they can divide their time in a way that allows them to prepare over long periods for the planting and harvesting. Those who depend more on row or paddy crops find themselves tied more constantly to the tending of these crops.

Pastoralists can have similarly characteristic approaches to time management and scheduling, depending upon the animals they're tending. A dairy farmer is with cattle every day: he milks them, he's home with his family and his social structure is built around a fixed home and family. Yet a cattle rancher, or cowboy, though working with the same domestic animal, will have a very different orientation to work, home, family, and territory. It's not just the animal; it's what you're trying to do with the animal.

Differences, too, in the physiology of the animals have implications for our discussion here. Sheep, goats, and bovines are ruminants with multiple-chambered stomachs. That means they can digest cellulose, a very tough substance to digest. It means they can tolerate more difficult grazing areas for example, than, horses. Discussing horses brings up the issue of attitudes toward territory and land ownership, and how attitudes towards those issues can be shaped differently by domesticates. Unlike animals that are excellent digesters of cellulose and can find enough nutrition from relatively poor grazing, horses are relatively inefficient grazers on poor-quality forage. This means that sheep, goats, and bovines can stay happy and healthy longer on a single spot of land. Horses, however, must move or be moved to "greener pastures," particularly if you hit periods of drought or periods when forage just does not come back. They have to be essentially moved off the land sometimes more frequently than cattle, goats, or sheep. You do understand that there are other factors that would play into this: It would depend on stocking rates—if you pile a whole bunch of sheep into a pasture they're going to eat it down and be hard up for food, too—but if you're talking about spreading these animals relatively evenly over the landscape, if things start to get tough, the ruminants are going to hang on better than the horses.

Horse tenders continually needed, then, new grazing lands to suit their animals' nutritional needs. Throughout history, tenders of horses were inclined to form mounted cavalries, because not only did they have to move their horses, the horses gave them this wonderful opportunity. This, in turn, stimulated technological advancement to make the horse an even more formidable weapon. Compound bows, stirrups, chariots, and war wagons: all the accoutrements of the use of horses in military activities. People who had horses had those opportunities; people who were not connected with horses: not so much an opportunity in that area.

This is another example of the way the domesticates we raise can influence the way our cultures form and develop. Look at some of the incursions by Mongols into parts of western Europe. We tend to attribute their attitude, bellicosity, and aggression to a sort of genetic difference, but I don't think that's really the case. On the Eurasian steppe, sheepherding cultures often measured wealth and status by the size of the flock under management. A person on foot, with the help of a trained herding dog, can manage effectively about 200 sheep as a full-time occupation. However, that same person and dog could manage over twice that many if the man could be mounted on horseback. Such larger flocks mean more status and wealth, but they also demand more range, as we just mentioned. That could lead to conflict at the borders between neighbors' lands. In order to deal with such armed competition, alliances needed to be formed; it was better to form allies and treaties than to fight it out over every little conflict. These were often cemented—these relationships—with elaborate feasts and extravagant gifts. Thus, these things get built into the fabric of the culture and it becomes a kind of ethnic icon. Some people have a tendency to want to have feasts, big events, make alliances that way, and do business over meals, things of that sort; others find that quite foreign, and it all traces back to what we were raising and what we were depending on.

It isn't a difference, in my opinion, in DNA between the sheep farmer who thinks of life in terms of one place for a 50 year stretch as opposed to the horse farmer-warrior; it has to do with the interplay of the culture with the domesticates. Over several generations, these needs of the domesticates defined not only the nature of the people who tended them directly, but the larger cultures that were comprised of those people. We have a sense of ourselves: Different areas of our country are rural or urban, and we have formed very specific ideas about the characteristics of people who come from each. Sometimes these different circumstances cause different attributes in the humans involved to be valued or devalued in different ways. I want to suggest that it is the interaction of humans with different domesticates that is largely responsible for many of our cultural and ethnic differences.

Even the kinds of gods worshiped can be affected by the domesticates with which people partner. This is certainly not an absolute situation, but I have noticed that ancient cultures that depend heavily on horticultural activities generally worship fertility gods that are usually female. However, a number of pastoralist cultures seemed to worship male gods that might have represented the male contributions to the herding practice, while those female gods represented fertility and fertility of the Earth.

As you know, one of the most obvious features of cultural identity and ethnicity is food. We know that from our own experience in a country composed of immigrants from many different ethnic groups. Long after these people have given up their language and their native dress, they still want to cling to their food culture. I know that from firsthand experience. Getting that food they are so connected with would have occupied a major portion of the time of these people; and again, the traits, desires, and preferences that come from the way one gets that food sets people apart and established ethnic identity.

In this first part of the course, I think we have pretty well established now that the foundations of civilization as we know it have their roots in the domestication of certain plants and animals. As our population grew, it had to be fed; as it had to be fed, we had to produce more food; and as we settled the land in order to produce larger quantities of food, the places we stayed, the climate, the nature of the land, and our plant and animal partners shaped our human culture as much as we shaped their evolving nature. It has been a 2-way coming together of humans and domesticates with both and each of them adapting and shaping their evolution to the other for the purpose of survival and continuity.

By way of review, let's go over a few things that we've covered today. One, we know that we've changed domesticates; that's a much-repeated point in this course. But what emerged in this lecture more clearly is that the domesticates we relied upon also changed us. We pointed out that different domesticates required different kind of care and different responses from human beings. We also mentioned that cultures struggle to succeed, and they will reward human behaviors and traits that enhance that survivability; they will discourage traits that work against it. This has led to cultural and even ethnic differences. These differences, coming so late in the development of modern humans, are probably a great deal more cultural than they are genetic.

With the next lecture, we're going to begin a review of the history and development of our oldest and most reliable domesticates. Bear in mind the ways that humans have both changed and have been changed by the mutual reliance we have had on one another. We will see you then.

Lecture Seven
The Domestication of Cereal Grains

Scope:

This is the first of several lectures on the history of the most successful plant and animal domesticates. Since plants and plant material are relatively easy to gather, it is likely the human diet has always contained a significant amount of vegetable matter—grains, fruits, and vegetables. We discuss wheat, barley, oats, corn, rice, and rye—rich, nutritious foods without which we would not have the population size we do today.

Outline

I. Cereal grains are annual plants that expend significant amounts of energy in reproduction and thus form relatively large seeds.

II. The progenitors of the 3 major types of wheat all grow wild in the Fertile Crescent.

   A. The first of the 3 types to be domesticated, einkorn wheat, is today used primarily as animal feed.

   B. Einkorn hybridizes naturally with one of its diploid wild relatives to form the tetraploid wheat called emmer wheat. Emmer is very useful in the making of noodles and pasta.

   C. Emmer also hybridizes with related wild diploids to form a hexaploid wheat called bread wheat, which is used extensively in fine baked goods and is the most important of the wheats in terms of human consumption.

   D. Norman Borlaug won the Nobel Peace Prize in 1970 for his work in developing a higher-yield wheat to help fight world hunger and starvation.

III. Barley was domesticated first in the Fertile Crescent at about the same time as einkorn wheat.

   A. Barley is more salt tolerant than most wheat. For that reason, it was grown in the southern part of the Tigris Euphrates valley after salinization became a problem.

B. Barley was at first used as a staple, but was probably always considered a poor substitute for wheat, since it does not make a good bread flour. It was widely used as animal feed, as it is today.

C. Barley is adaptable to a greater range of climates than any other grain. It is also able to grow and ripen faster than any of the other cereals.

D. There is good evidence that Roman gladiators ate large amounts of barley to add bulk to their bodies.

E. Early on, it was discovered that barley could be malted and brewed, thus turning it from a low-quality grain into a high-quality beverage.

F. Although other grains can be fermented into alcohol, barley is the most commonly used. It has a large amount of the 2 enzymes necessary for starch breakdown.

G. Today more than 10% of the world's barley is used for malt.

IV. The wild progenitor of oats grows in the Middle East, but it was never effectively domesticated there.

A. Oats probably reached Europe as a contaminant in a shipment of wheat.

B. They probably grew as a weed in Europe for some time before being domesticated in central Europe about 3000 years ago.

C. From there, oats spread quickly to regions that were too cool for optimum cultivation of wheat.

D. Oats make wonderful straw.

E. Oats are second only to rye in survivability in poor soils.

V. Rice is one of the most important staple crops in the world, accounting for a significant portion of the caloric intake of much of the world's population.

A. There is some controversy about the origins of domestic rice.

    1. Some favor an Indian origin, while others feel China is the initial domestication site.

    2. The rice genome is not easily studied. It is complex, and there are many small chromosomes. It may actually contain more genes than the human genome.

3. The picture is clouded further by the fact that the wild progenitors may have had a very broad distribution before domestication.

4. The unusually large number of cultivars and types in current use also adds complexity to the study of the origin of the first domesticated strain.

B. There are several main types of rice, including African rice and Asian, or paddy, rice. The plant we call wild rice in the United States is not a close relative to Asian or African rice.

VI. Maize was domesticated in Mexico or Guatemala from a wild progenitor called teosinte.

A. American farmers had greatly modified the plant by the time the Europeans reached the New World in the late 15th century.

B. At that time, maize was in cultivation from what today is Argentina all the way to southern Canada.

C. That plant, though much smaller and producing smaller ears than modern hybrid maize, more closely resembled the modern plant than it did teosinte.

VII. These 5—wheat, barley, oats, rice, and corn—are the main cereal grains consumed by the people of the world, but there is another grain that should be mentioned, too: rye.

A. Rye was found as a weed widely distributed in wheat and barley fields in southern Asia sometime around 1800 B.C.

B. In Europe, rye became a staple for bread but was considered inferior to wheat bread, which was a luxury food.

C. Today we know that rye reduces soil erosion and enhances water penetration and retention and thus fits well in erosion control strategies.

VIII. It is interesting that out of all the plants available to our hunter-gatherer ancestors, we rely on a relatively small number of grains to sustain such a significant percentage of the human population.

Suggested Reading:

Chrispeels and Sadava, *Plants, Food, and People*, chap. 6.

Hancock, *Plant Evolution*, chap. 8.

Questions to Consider:

1. Why do you think wheat has played such an important role in the spread of Western civilization? What advantages would it have had over other cereal grains that would account for this?

2. What properties of a wheat plant would make it the most desirable to early practitioners of agriculture?

3. Wheat became a staple in the Western world because of its remarkable utility. Do you think this increased or decreased the food security of the populations of Europe and the Middle East?

4. Cereal grains make up a significant portion of the world's total calorie intake. To what do you attribute that?

Lecture Seven—Transcript
The Domestication of Cereal Grains

Hello; and welcome back as we begin a new direction in this course. In this section of the course, I'd like to discuss the history of some of the most successful of our plant and animal domesticates. We're going to start with the plants. Animals, after all, are mobile and possess various defense mechanisms against predators; but since plants and plant material are relatively easy to gather—they're more accessible—it is likely that the human diet has always contained a significant amount of vegetable matter: grains, fruits, and vegetables. We're going to discuss wheat, barley, oats, corn, rice, and rye in this lecture. These are rich, nutritious foods, without which we—human beings—would not have the population numbers that we have today.

Collectively, the cereals provide a significant portion of the total caloric intake of the world population. Wheat, barley, oats, and rye are all Old World products. Corn is a New World plant, and rice, though certainly from somewhere in Asia, does have rather uncertain origins as we'll discuss later. The ancestors of these grains appealed to our hunter-gather forebears who picked the seeds best suited to their needs, and after many hundreds of years they succeeded in creating domesticated forms that best suited their needs and ours. Today, these few plants comprise the bulk of the plant-based calories our species consumes. These grains come to us one of 2 different ways: Of course, they can come either as their whole grain form, or they can come to us passed through animal products, because animals are also animals nourished on some of these same grains, and we, when we consume the animal products, are getting those grains kind of second hand. Scientists continue to select and manipulate the cultivation of them in new ways, ways that our ancestors obviously could never have dreamed of, in order to try to satisfy the very many hungry mouths of our world today. We'll talk more about that in a later lecture.

Cereal grains are what we call annual plants; they have to be reseeded each year. They expend significant amounts of energy in reproduction and thus they tend to form relatively large seeds; not necessarily huge, but relatively large seeds. As stated in the first lecture of this course, this property, along with the relative ease of gathering and storing, may have been what first attracted our hunter-gatherer ancestors to these plants. The oldest of these may well be wheat, which, according to the archaeological evidence we find, has actually been under cultivation for over 9000 years, 9 millennia. The progenitors of the 3—and there are 3—major types of wheat all grow in the Fertile Crescent. In order to make sense of the sequence of domestication events that had to take place to establish these 3 main types of domesticated wheat, we'll need to spend just a very few minutes talking about the organization of the genetic material in the nuclei of plants and animals. We'll cover briefly things such as cell division, meiosis, and mitosis, chromosomes and chromosome number. Please understand I will be mindful that this is not a course in elementary biology.

The first thing to keep in mind is that our domesticated plants and our domesticated animals are what we call eukaryotes; they are macroscopic organisms, and they have cells that contain a true nucleus, a membrane-bounded nucleus. The bulk of the genetic material, the DNA, of these creatures is contained within that membrane-bounded nucleus. Most of the time that DNA is dispersed and unwound and it's busily being expressed to produce the organism's phenotype. But when the cells get ready to divide, they can't have all that loose DNA so the DNA compresses and tightens up into these little stick-like structures called chromosomes that can easily be observed in a light microscope. One of the first things people realized when they began to look at these chromosomes under the microscope was that they tended to be in even numbers and that they formed pairs; that there would always be 2 that would look alike, and so you could sort of line them up in pairs. When cells get ready to divide in ordinary cell division, just before the division each of the chromosomes divides and the mechanism separates the 2 daughter cells in such a way that each of the daughters receives exactly the right amount of DNA in exactly the right number of chromosomes in exactly the right number of pairs.

But in one special kind of cell division called meiosis, we don't make new body cells, we make sex cells. In our parlance, that usually means we're talking about sperms and eggs. What happens there, just before the division, the DNA and the chromosomes do not divide, and instead of pairs being separated, the pairs are actually pulled apart. This is called a reductive division, and so the sex cells have half as many chromosomes as the typical body cells; the number has been reduced. That means, then, that a sperm has not a bunch of pairs of chromosomes but it has a bunch of single chromosomes looking for other ones to make a pair; an egg the same way. In fertilization when they come together, pairs are reunited, and that's the moment, then, of fertilization.

We can talk, then, about chromosome number; and the simplest, easiest way to think about things: Just think about the body cell of a plant or an animal; we will usually call that the $2n$ or diploid number, meaning that the chromosomes are in pairs (duplicates, diploid number). In sex cells, we have the $1n$ number, or the haploid number. But occasionally, particularly in the world of plants but it can happen in animals, sometimes cells will fuse in hybridizations bringing in whole new genomes, and then you would not have just one pair of each kind of chromosome you might have another set of pairs, and that would give you a $4n$ number, or the tetraploid. You might get yet another set of these coming in and that would give you a chromosome number of 6, and you'd call that a hexaploid. That's the end of our beginning biology lesson.

The first of the 3 wheat types to be domesticated is called einkorn. Today einkorn wheat is used almost exclusively as an animal feed. But interestingly, einkorn hybridizes naturally with one of its diploid wild relatives; now you have diploid einkorn hybridizing with a diploid relative to make emmer wheat. Emmer is a very useful wheat in making things like noodles and pasta; the well-known Semolina flour is one of a number of varieties of this kind of wheat. Emmer also can hybridize with related wild diploids to form a hexaploid; so now you have 3 kinds of wheat with 3 different chromosome numbers: einkorn (diploid), emmer (tetraploid), and now this new one (hexaploid) that has a really original name, bread wheat. Not surprising, it's the one that's used for fine baking and, of course, is primarily used for making the so-called "staff of life," it's used in making bread. It is the most important of the various wheats in terms of human consumption.

We continue to work with this amazing grain even today. The scientist Norman Borlaug won the Nobel Prize in 1970 for his work in developing a higher-yielding wheat to help fight world hunger and starvation. It's worth noting that the Nobel Prize given to Borlaug was for world peace, it was not a scientific award, because the Nobel committee recognized, fully understood, that by feeding people and removing hunger Borlaug was clearly working toward world peace. That work involving not only plant breeding, but also based on teaching people in developing regions the basics of agronomy and plant breeding, was the start of what was later called the Green Revolution and may have been responsible for increasing the carrying capacity of those regions where it was employed for human beings; more human beings in those regions because food became substantially less limiting.

Barley was first domesticated in the Fertile Crescent at about the same time as einkorn wheat. You may recall that in a previous lecture we noted that barley is more salt tolerant than most wheat. Remember what that was about? We were talking about irrigation in the Tigris-Euphrates Valley. For that reason it was grown in the southern part of the Tigris-Euphrates valley after salinization became a problem; and that salinization was caused by the particular method of irrigation that people at the time were using. The ground became more saline, and then barley got to be introduced rather than wheat. It was at first used as a staple, but was probably always considered a sort of poor substitute for wheat since it does not make a good bread flour. It was widely used for animal feed, as much of it is yet today. Barley is adaptable to a greater range of climate than any other grain. It's also able to grow and ripen faster than any of the other cereal grains; so it has some real positive attributes. There is good evidence that Roman gladiators also ate large amounts of barley to add bulk to their bodies because they were frequently wounded and they needed to heal, and having bulk helped them in many ways.

Early on, it was discovered that barley could be malted and brewed, thus turning it from a low-quality grain into a high-quality beverage. Although other grains can be fermented into alcohol and beers, barley is the most commonly-used. It has a large amount of 2 enzymes necessary for starch breakdown; starch is a polymer of individual sugar units. These enzymes are called the alpha and beta amylases. They break the starch polymers down to individual glucose molecules that are actually the starting point for the alcoholic fermentation that is catalyzed by another organism: yeast. No other grain is capable of more amylolytic activity. Even in wheat beers, which are now becoming quite popular—that is, beers that contain a significant amount of wheat—barley malt is still a major component because the brewers want that amylolytic activity to break down the wheat starch as well. Barley is also most useful for beer making among the other grains because it has no particular husk around its seeds; also the nature of its starch granules is particularly conducive to that malting process; and there are some other variables that have to do, I think, with the fact that we've gotten used to barley in beer and so we like the flavors and the other properties that it produces. Today more than 10% of the world's barley is used for malt, but I'll tell you I'd be one unhappy person if I couldn't find just some barley to use regularly in my own lamb stews.

The wild progenitor of oats grows in the Middle East, but it was never effectively domesticated there. This is one of those anomalies that would not have worked well in the biological approach developed by Vavilov that was discussed one of our earlier lectures. Oats probably reached Europe as a contaminant in a shipment of wheat. It probably grew as a weed in Europe for some time before being domesticated—probably before anybody paid attention to it—and that domestication took place about 3000 years ago, probably in central Europe. From there, it spread quickly to regions that were too cool for optimum cultivation of wheat. Oats make wonderful straw, and if this lecture was being given 35 years ago I wouldn't even think about defining straw; but some people I know now, because we're primarily urbanized, mix up straw and hay. Hay is a whole plant cut off at the ground, usually dried, baled, or chopped up and used for animal feed. Straw is the stem of a grain that's left after the seeds are taken off, and it makes very good bedding for animals but it also used to be good for stuffing mattresses, for padding clothing, and it tends to be rather clean, it's a good insulator, and it's soft.

Oats are second only to rye in survivability in poor soils. In 1887, Quaker Oats was the first registered trademark for a breakfast cereal in the United States. I find that interesting because I was born and raised in Cedar Rapids, Iowa where Quaker Oats operated what was for years the world's largest cereal mill; I still remember looking at it.

Rice is one of the most important staple crops in the world, accounting for a significant portion of the caloric intake of a large portion of the world's population. There is some controversy about the origins of domestic rice. Some favor an Indian origin, while others feel China is the initial domestication site. There are some problems, though, in figuring this out, because the rice genome is not easily studied. It is complex and there are many small chromosomes in the nucleus. It may actually contain—some people have said this—more genes than the human genome; but I think that could be a definitional issue depending on how we want to define a gene. The picture is clouded further by the fact that the wild progenitors may have had a very broad distribution before the point of domestication. Again, this is a weakness in the biological method pioneered by Vavilov, which works best if you have a tightly contained range for the wild progenitor. The unusually large number of cultivars and types in current use also adds another level of complexity to the study of the origin of the first domesticated strain. There are several main types of rice including African rice or Asian rice that we call paddy rice. The plant that we call "wild rice" in America is not a close relative to either Asian or African rice.

Those are Old World plants; now let's turn our attention to maize, a New World grain. Maize was domesticated either in Mexico or Guatemala from a wild progenitor called teosinte. American farmers had greatly modified the plant by the time the Europeans reached the New World in the late 15th century. At that time, maize was in cultivation from what today is Argentina all the way to Southern Canada. That plant, though much smaller and producing smaller ears than modern hybrid maize, more closely resembled the modern plant than it did teosinte. There was a long-running controversy in the world of plant genetics concerning the true progenitor of maize. Because teosinte looks so very different from maize, a number of scientists felt that it just could not be the progenitor. But a scientist named George Beadle and a group of his colleagues eventually amassed enough evidence in favor of the teosinte theory that it is now generally accepted as corn's wild ancestor. Beadle is probably best known for his Nobel Prize-winning work on gene expression that was one of the first things that showed how the genotype begat the phenotype; or, in other words, how genes expressed form and function. He later became the president of the University of Chicago, and was well-known to a different group of non-scientist Americans because he's the person who eliminated the game of football from the University of Chicago.

The world of maize agriculture in America has a number of interesting participants. One of the most interesting was a fellow named Lester Pfister. This farmer, Mister Pfister, became the biggest United States individual grower of hybrid seed corn. Remember, this is seed corn; not corn that people are going to eat but corn that people are going to plant. In 1948, his company pushed the national average yield of corn, once only 25 bushels per acre, to a record 42.7 bushels. In Pfister's own county, the yield was 66 bushels per acre;

that's a lot of corn. A farm boy who quit school in the eighth grade to work in the cornfields at $30 a month, he began inbreeding and crossbreeding corn in 1925. His neighbors, watching him tie little paper bags over the corn tassels and ear shoots to control pollination, called him "Crazy Lester." To keep up his experiments, he mortgaged everything he owned. When the Depression then hit, he stalled off bankruptcy only by outrunning and evading his creditors. One day after that he went to an El Paso bank to plead for a last-ditch loan. Unwrapping a newspaper, he produced a 10-inch ear of corn, the best that any of the people in that boardroom had seen; the best ever grown by a Woodford County farmer. He then, when they were looking at that, unwrapped a handsome 14-inch ear of Pfister corn grown from hybrid seed. He got the loan; and by the age of 51, Pfister was the president and major stockholder of a bank which had once refused him a loan. As a boy growing up in Iowa, I often made extra spending money by doing corn detasseling—we didn't tie little bags on it anymore, we actually pulled the tassels off—which is part of the process in making hybrid seed corn; so I feel some small connection to Crazy Lester.

Today, maize is widely cultivated on several continents and provides a significant portion of the caloric content of a large portion of the world's population, it serves as a very high quality animal feed, and now may find new uses in the manufacture of biofuels; I'll say a little bit more about that in a moment. It provides the sweetening agent for a vast number of the "non-diet" carbonated beverages available worldwide, and is also a very common sweetener in a major portion of all processed foods. Because of its high sugar content and ease of harvest, it was recognized early as a great starting material for what are known as sour mash whiskeys. In a process similar to the alcoholic fermentation in beer, the sugar in corn mash is anaerobically fermented by yeast to ethanol and CO_2. It therefore stands to reason that it could be a good feed stock for anaerobic production of ethanol to be used as a biofuel. This is a hot topic in political, economic, and environmental circles.

Why is it a hot topic? First of all, you could argue that maybe we don't need that much additional biofuel. Second, it's expensive to produce it, and it only makes economic sense if petroleum becomes very expensive; then there's a niche that it can fit into. But one of the big problems is that these plants that make ethanol are not nice to live around: they have nasty odors, they consume a lot of water, they consume a lot of energy, and they produce a lot of by-product, again, that doesn't smell particularly good. Also, we are using land to grow corn for fuel that could be used to grow corn or other things for food; and so here we have that problem we've mentioned so many times: You either use the land more intensely or you use more of it; and now we're using some of it for biofuel, and what does that do? It drives up the cost of food and makes food less readily available.

We have these 5: wheat, barley, oats, corn, and rice. They are the main cereal grains consumed by the people of the world. But there is another grain that should be mentioned, too, and that is rye. Rye was found as a weed widely distributed in wheat and barley fields in southern Asia sometime around 1800 B.C., so almost 4000 years ago. In Europe, rye became a staple for bread, but was considered inferior to wheat bread, which was a luxury food; we know that from literature that the dark bread was sort of the people's bread and the hoi polloi ate white bread made from bread wheat. We just talked about that: hexaploid wheat. Today, we've found that rye reduces soil erosion, and it does something else very important: It enhances water penetration into the soil and retention; thus rice fits very well into a number of new soil erosion control strategies.

It's interesting to note that out of all the many plants available to our hunter-gatherer ancestors, we rely upon a relatively small number of grains to sustain such a huge percent of the human population. Much of the total caloric consumption of our total word population is taken care of by those major grains. But there are other, less commonly-known or used grains such as amaranth, buckwheat, millet, spelt, teff, quinoa, and others more popular in parts of the world other than the United States, and they are becoming better-known and more widely available for a very interesting reason: A lot of health-conscious people now are beginning to realize that whole grains bring some real benefits to the diet. You can go to the store and how many times do you see something that's called "5 grain," or "7 grain," or "9 grain" bread or crackers or something of that sort? Some of you probably sat there and tried to figure out, "Do I know the name of 5 or 7 or 9 grains?" That's what some of these are being used for, and I think they are adding vitamins, minerals, and soluble fiber; they're adding interest and variety to the basic American diet.

We've discussed before the fact that the domestication of plants and animals was a 2-way street; that in order for domestication to occur, both the domesticate and the humans had to meet each other halfway. The selection of which plants to domesticate had to do with several factors: the specific needs of the plant, that is, the soil make-up, the amount of water, the climate, the amount of sun (that's important); as well as the specific needs of the human, and what would those be? Ease of harvest, ease of storage and processing, digestibility, nutritive qualities, and having a relatively high calorie-efficient yield. There were, again, reasons from both sides.

In our next lecture, we will discuss the domestication of some of the more important groups of garden vegetables. We'll see here, also, that the list is a relatively—and surprisingly, I think—a short one, given all of the various plants available to choose from. Each of these lectures keeps emphasizing a point that was made early in this course: Our ancient ancestors made some very good choices in picking the plants and animals they wished to partner with. That may have been due in no small part to which plants or animals met us halfway on the way to domestication. But in this process, we began to depend more and more on this relatively small number of organisms to provide our nourishment and we began to forget about many of the other options that may have at one time been available. The end result for us is that our diets are actually narrower than we might imagine with the bulk of our nourishment coming from a relatively small number of fairly closely-related creatures. We will take up that subject next time.

Lecture Eight
The Oligarchy of the Garden Patch

Scope:

We rely on a fairly small group of domesticated plants for our food. None are particularly difficult to grow, and you may have actually cultivated some of them in your family garden. Let's discuss the histories of—and learn some surprising tidbits about—these foods.

Outline

I. There are thousands of wild plants that have the potential to be domesticated. Let's look at the limited number of plant families that much of our food comes from.

II. Let's talk first about the legume family, which is composed of dicotyledonous plants that typically carry their seeds in some sort of pod.

   A. Soybean, peanut, common bean, and cowpea are major sources of dietary protein and calories for human consumption in much of the world, but not in the United States.

   B. Many members of this group are capable of a mutualistic relationship with the nodule-forming bacterium *Rhizobium*, which results in nitrogen fixation.

   C. Legumes play a vital role in vegetarian diets.

   D. Some legumes can be made into secondary products, such as peanut butter, candy, humus, and tofu.

III. The Solanaceae family of plants has long been known to herbalists and agriculturists.

   A. The Solanaceae family is very important economically and includes potatoes, tomatoes, eggplant, and peppers and is closely allied to coffee.

   B. Its plants tend to have thick, fleshy stems.

IV. The Cole family includes such important plants as oil-seed rape (canola), turnips, Chinese cabbage (bok choi), rutabaga, black mustard, brown mustard, and Ethiopian mustard.

  A. Some of its members are the result of both natural and artificial selection favoring one part or the other of the plant to provide a specialized vegetable.

  B. Some members, like cabbages and kales, were probably used for medicinal purposes before being cultivated for food.

V. The last group in our domesticated plant families is the cucurbits.

  A. The cucurbits come in a variety of different types, such as squash, melons, gourds, pumpkins, and cucumbers.

  B. There is evidence that many of these plants have been under domestication for many millennia in the New World.

VI. If we take an imaginary trip around our neighborhood supermarket, focusing only on the plant materials, we realize that there are actually a small number of plants—processed, prepared, and packaged in different ways—giving the illusion of great variety. Our diet is not as varied as we think it is.

Suggested Reading:

Albala, *Beans*, chaps. 1–2.

Chrispeels and Sadava, *Plants, Food, and People*, chap. 3.

Creasy, *The Edible Heirloom Garden*, 21–57.

Hancock, *Plant Evolution*, chaps. 9–11.

Questions to Consider:

1. What is there about the biology of the legume group that has caused it to be labeled the "poor man's meat"?

2. Entering a modern supermarket, one gets the impression of great choice and variety. Have you ever considered making a list of the number of different plant species you are actually filling your grocery cart with? You might find it an interesting exercise.

3. Think about cabbage, kale, Brussels sprouts, cauliflower, kohlrabi, and broccoli. Given that these vegetables were all derived from the same progenitor, can you hazard a guess as to how plant breeders derived so many seemingly different vegetables from one plant?

Lecture Eight—Transcript
The Oligarchy of the Garden Patch

Welcome. In the last lecture, I made the point that agricultural societies utilize a smaller number of plant species than did their hunting-gathering predecessors. What is even more surprising is the degree to which that already small number falls into an even smaller number of plant families or groups. Therefore, I've titled this lecture "The Oligarchy of the Garden Patch" to signify that a few prominent families occupy much of the space in our gardens or supermarkets. The fact that I can cover a very large percentage of all the plant food, except for the tree fruit and nuts, found in the fresh produce section of a typical grocery store in a single lecture should highlight the fact that we rely upon a fairly small group of domesticated plants for our food. Each of these foods has a special history and a surprising tidbit or 2. Many of them you or family members of yours may have actually cultivated in a family garden. None are particularly difficult to grow with some focused effort on soil quality, pest control, and watering, and in some cases—like, for example, cauliflower—a little bit of light management.

There are literally thousands of wild plants that have the potential to be domesticated. Hunter-gatherers in fertile regions often used many dozens of these plants without domesticating them. Some people who practice forest "grazing" or some who are interested in survival techniques still utilize some of these plant sources that can be quite nutritious and add variety and valuable nutrition to the diet. But after the Neolithic Revolution and the widespread domestication of plants, human beings came to rely on a much, much smaller number of highly productive and relatively easily-cultivatable domesticated plants. Many of these plants are rather closely related, and come from a limited number of plant families. They account for a large percentage of the plants currently under cultivation for food outside those grain staples that we talked about before. Of course, the grains, as you know, provide a major portion of the caloric intake for the majority of the world's people, but these plants we'll talk about today fill a lot of other gaps.

Let's talk first about the legume family which is composed of dicotyledonous plants—they have 2 cotyledons that open up when the seeds germinate—that typically carry their seeds in some kind of a pod; like peapods or bean pods, something of that sort. What are these plants? Soybean, peanut, the common beans, and cowpea are major sources of dietary protein and calories for human consumption in much of the world, but interestingly, not so much in the United States. Most, but, of course, by no means all Americans still get much of their dietary protein from animal sources: meat, milk and other dairy products, fish, and shellfish; but in much of the world those things are not so readily available. Carbonized remains suggest that peas, lentils, and chickpeas were domesticated in the Near East and were cultivated with the cereals as early as about 9000 years ago; and, of course, those things are still in the diets of people from those regions. From there, it's assumed that peas spread to the cool-temperate areas of central and northern Europe and from there were introduced into the western hemisphere soon after Columbus reached the New World; and we'll be talking about that in detail later.

Many members of this group are capable of a mutualistic symbiotic relationship with the nodule-forming bacterium, *Rhizobium*, which results in nitrogen fixation that's a really important concept to grasp. We're going to talk just a little bit about this special property that the legumes have in association with a bacterium called *Rhizobium* to carry out the process of nitrogen fixation. It's important to actually take a few minutes and talk about that because it is so critical to nutrition, agronomy, the health of the world's population, and the health of our soils. It's also a very interesting story because it shows a great interplay between 2 unrelated organisms for mutual benefit.

Let's start with the concept of nitrogen. Nitrogen is an important element in the molecules that make up the bodies of plants and animals. For example, DNA is rich in nitrogen, proteins are rich in nitrogen, and a number of vitamins contain nitrogen; so it's an important element. That's not too surprising, because why? We live on planet Earth, and we have an atmosphere that has a load of nitrogen in it; we are walking around in a veritable sea of nitrogen. But remember from your early chemistry, probably in high school, that when you were told about nitrogen you were told that it was an inert gas; and for all intents and purposes, it is inert to us. If you have a nitrogen deficiency, don't bother trying to resolve it by breathing deeply; you cannot utilize the molecular nitrogen in the atmosphere. That might not surprise you, but this probably will: No eukaryotic organism can use that nitrogen in the atmosphere directly. Eukaryotes have lost the capacity to do that; so all plants and all animals that are eukaryotes—the macroscopic creatures with which we are so familiar—have to have a source of reduced or fixed nitrogen. The reservoir for nitrogen on the planet is that atmosphere; so how do we get nitrogen into the food chain? We're pretty clever creatures; we figured out how to do it in our advanced civilization, we have something called the Haber process. We can take nitrogen gas, put it in a strong tank, exert tremendous pressure, and heat it to a very high temperature; and voila, we can produce ammonia. The Haber process; very energy-expensive, but it produces a lot of our nitrogen fertilizers.

But biological symbiotic nitrogen fixation carried out by the legumes and their partners the *Rhizobium* bacterium do this at ambient temperature and pressure; it's quite a trick. All of the nitrogen coming out of the reservoir in the atmosphere into the food chain—into the biome, if you will—has to come by way of the action of prokaryotes (microorganisms; creatures that don't have true nuclei). You talk about being an interconnected and interdependent planet; we're on it. How does this process work? The prokaryotes are living free in the soil, the *Rhizobium*. You plant the legume, its roots go down, and little root hairs extend out, and when they contact a *Rhizobium*, the *Rhizobium* infects, it goes into the root hairs. The plant responds: It walls off the invading, if you will, *Rhizobium*; it builds this little nodule. The *Rhizobium* could live in the atmosphere, but to fix nitrogen it has to be in an anaerobic (oxygen-free) environment. The plant, not the bacterium, then makes this protein called leghemoglobin—it's much like our own hemoglobin, only it's made by a plant—and like our hemoglobin, it binds oxygen; it goes down into the nodules and it soaks up the oxygen, making the nodule anaerobic. The *Rhizobium* then begins to fix nitrogen that's, of course, diffused down into the soil from the atmosphere and it begins to produce reduced nitrogen that nourishes the plant; the plant now has all the nitrogen it needs, it doesn't need fertilizer. This is an effective enough process that actual nitrogen leaks out of the plant, enriches the soil around it, and can be used by other plants that aren't legumes and aren't doing this kind of symbiotic nitrogen fixation. It also, not surprisingly, leads to the production of seeds in the legumes that are rather rich in nitrogen compounds. It's quite a process.

It can often be more economical for a farmer to "inter seed" or crop rotate with a legume to fix nitrogen than it is to pay for nitrogen fertilizer often made with something like the Haber process. In my own case, I inter seed my own pastures which virtually eliminates the need to use commercial fertilizers in a system like mine where the animals range free and deposit their wastes on the pasture. If I were in a production system and not in a breeding system, and I was taking large numbers of animals off the pasture every year to go to make lamb chops, then I would be exporting a lot of nitrogen that started in the atmosphere, got fixed by the legumes, got put into the sheep when they ate it; I would be exporting it out to my customers that would eat the lamb, and so when that happens you do have to fertilize. But in my case, I take only a few animals off, and so I can leave the pasture as it is, and that allows things to remain enriched for nitrogen without having to add fertilizer.

The ability of legumes, then, to fix nitrogen can save us money, it can reduce our dependence on petroleum products, and it improves the soil and the water quality. As I mentioned, a consequence of this nitrogen fixation process is that many of these plants produce seeds that have a rather high protein content. In areas where meat is scarce, members of this group are often referred to as "poor man's meat." Why? Because they're supplying nitrogen; and when we eat meat, that's one of the things we primarily want to get: the nitrogen compounds out of the meat; we want the amino acids to build our own proteins. Legumes play a vital role in vegetarian diets for that same reason. Legumes that are commonly eaten are all the beans and peas, soybeans, of course, peanuts, chickpeas, and lentils. Some of these plants can be made into secondary products like peanut butter and a number of different kinds of candy, humus, tofu, and in addition to tofu a wide range of other products and additives made from soy, some of which are found actually in the dairy aisle, in the processed food aisle, and even in various canned foods. You don't always find this stuff in the produce section.

Protein content in the field pea, chickpea, and lentil is roughly 20%; that's high. These legumes are popular in the Near East and North Africa. They're a mainstay in the Indian Subcontinent, and especially where religious preferences forbid eating meat. It should be noted if you're a vegetarian or a vegan that there are no plant proteins, even from these wonderful legumes, that are what we call complete proteins; so it is very important to be sure if you've taken animal products out of your diet to eat an appropriate balance of these legumes and other high-protein plants so that in combination you get the equivalent of eating complete proteins like you would get from eating animal products.

The Solanaceae family of plants has long been known to herbalists and agriculturists. It includes more than 3000 species. Many evolved in South America, and the center of diversity is very near the equator. Several species were therefore undisturbed when those ice sheets came down during those ice ages, and when they receded and the plants moved that way with them they had time to accumulate adaptive genetic variation for extreme conditions. The Solanaceae is a very important plant family economically and includes a number of things: potatoes, tomatoes, eggplant, and peppers; and it's actually closely allied to coffee, but we won't put coffee into this lecture, we're not going to call it a member of the Solanaceae. All of these plants tend to have thick, fleshy stems. It's commonly known as the night-shade family, and it also includes some poisonous weeds and shrubs, and some pharmaceutically very important plants. Belladonna is a plant well-known to European herbalists, and its resemblance in growth mode to other members of the Solanaceae has resulted in some members of the family actually being viewed with suspicion as food plants by people who know the other properties of some of the other Solanaceae. Belladonna is the source of the drug atropine, which is a poison if taken in high dose, but which is very important medically and couple of its uses are to combat convulsions and to dilate the pupil of the eye; so many of us have encountered atropine.

The progenitors of tomatoes come from South America, but they were not domesticated there. Here we go again: This is yet another exception to the Vavilov biological approach that we discussed earlier. It's thought that birds carried tomato seeds in their guts and deposited them in the fields prepared for maize and gourds by Amerindian farmers in Mexico; another example of something we mentioned earlier: a plant dispersing its seeds by wrapping them in an attractive food source that an animal will eat and then carry the seeds away for dispersal. Then, in Mexico, they grew as weeds until some of those early Amerindian farmers appreciated their value and began to domesticate them through selective breeding and artificial selection. In North America, the tomato was believed to be poisonous until the mid-1800s, though it was grown often as an ornamental plant well before that for the nice look of the plant and the fruits.

The potato is another member of the Solanaceae plant family. Potatoes were first domesticated in the Andes, but now are also common in North America and in much of Europe; they're a good source for vodka, for example, in some parts of eastern Europe. The potato was first cultivated in South America between 3000 and 7000 years ago, though scientists believe they probably grew wild in that region as long as 13,000 years ago. The Incas had learned to preserve the potato for storage by actually dehydrating and mashing potatoes into a substance that could be stored at room temperature for up to 10 years, providing excellent insurance against possible crop failures. Potatoes were first introduced to the colonies in the 1620s, but they did not become widely accepted until they received an aristocratic seal of approval from none other than Thomas Jefferson, who served them to guests in the White House. They come in a very wide variety of sizes, shapes, colors, and textures—there are the waxy ones, the mealy ones, the yellow ones, the purple ones—but these tubers are not closely related to either sweet potatoes or yams, which are not members of the Solanaceae at all.

Eggplant is also a member of that family, and it has an Old World origin, while, of course, tomatoes are New World plants. Eggplant was probably first domesticated in the Indo-Burma region; the earliest record of domesticated eggplant goes back to the 1st century B.C. World production of this plant exceeds 31 million tons a year, and the leading producers are China, India, Egypt, Turkey—all quite reasonable given where it was first domesticated—but also Japan and Italy; both countries where it figures prominently in the local or regional cuisines. The word "eggplant" dates to the British occupation of India where that variety of eggplant that is white and sort of egg-shaped was popular; so the English colonials began to call it "eggplant." But ironically, when you go to England today, what we call "eggplant" they call "aubergine"; there is a certain irony there, because we get the "eggplant" name from the raj in India.

Another member of this Solanaceae family, the peppers, or Capsicum group, are one of the most diverse plant groups on the whole planet. There are literally hundreds of different types of peppers under cultivation. If you think about it, you can name a bunch yourself: there are green ones, red ones, yellow ones, and orange ones; but there are also jalapeño peppers, ancho peppers, habaneros, and banana peppers. In the cuisines of most every region in the world you find peppers; imagine Hungarian cuisine without paprika which, of course, is a pepper. They have been a part of the human diet for over 9000 years. Columbus is given credit for introducing the chile to Europe, and subsequently to Africa and to

Asia. On his first voyage, he encountered a plant whose fruit mimicked the pungency of the black pepper; and remember, that's what Columbus was looking for. Columbus called it "red pepper" because the pods were red. Materials isolated from peppers are now being used as pharmaceuticals in, of all things, pain control, because they do burn, but they can, of course, fool the nerve endings in some kinds of chronic pain and can bring some relief. One of the compounds, capsicum, can now actually be purchased over the counter. Derivatives of this same chemical are the active ingredient in pepper spray that can be used for personal protection or in crowd control. Tobacco is also another member of this Solanaceae family, but we will discuss its special role in a later lecture.

The Cole family is the next group of domesticated plants we'll discuss, and a few of its members are the result of both natural and artificial selection favoring one part or the other of the same plant to provide a specialized vegetable. They are part of the genus *Brassica*. In this group, we find such important plants as oil-seed rape (of course, in America we can't say that so we call it "canola"), turnips, Chinese cabbage (bok choi), rutabaga, black mustard, brown mustard, and Ethiopian mustard. Cabbage and kales probably originated in western Europe and were the first coles to be domesticated. Before being cultivated for food, however, they were probably used for medicinal purposes, because all of these plants have a fairly high sulfur content, which early herbalists might have found interesting. Gardeners and plant breeders have been able to use artificial selection to produce cabbage, kohlrabi, cauliflower, kale, broccoli, and Brussels sprouts from a single species of this group, *Brassica oleracea*. What they essentially did was find mutants that favored one part or the other of the plant, either the sprout, the flower, the stem, or the leaf, and that's the way you get these different vegetables; it's essentially one plant pulled in different directions genetically. A number of secondary products are made from members of this family. Significant quantities of, of course, canola oil are produced from oil-seed rape. There is a rich selection of prepared mustards available from a number of different cultures and food traditions. Several important fermented secondary products such as sauerkraut and kimchee are produced from the various cabbages; these, of course, have long shelf lives.

I'd like to point out that we've discussed just 3 main groups now— the legumes, the Solanaceae, and the Coles—but consider the variety of edible materials we've just discussed. The last group in our domesticated plant families in this particular lecture is going to be the cucurbits. The cucurbits come in a variety of different types but can be usefully described as squash, melons, gourds, pumpkins, or cucumbers. There is evidence that many of these plants have been under domestication for many millennia in the New World. Of course, in fact, one member of this group, the bottle gourd, is likely the very first plant domesticate predating the actual Neolithic Revolution by several millennia. It was not domesticated as a food plant, as we mentioned, as much as it was as an item of convenience, well-suited to carrying water and other materials that could have been invaluable to hunter-gathers as they moved out of Africa. Cucumbers were probably first domesticated in India and gourds were first cultivated in Africa, but, as we've said, spread rapidly to other locations where they've been under cultivation for many thousands of years. The wild origins of these plants are know in some cases, but it is a complicated group with a very wide geographic distribution and obvious utility making the provenance of some of the modern cultivars extremely difficult to determine.

By way of an informal review of these lectures on the grains and the garden patch, let's now do one of our mind experiments: Let's take an imaginary trip around our neighborhood supermarket and take a look around at what's there. For now, let's focus only on the plant materials—we'll leave the animal products alone—available for purchase. When you enter this supermarket, what's your first impression? It's immediately one of an almost bewildering array of different products providing amazing choice to satisfy our modern "hunter-shopper" tendencies; we want to be "shopper-gatherers," I guess, when we go in those places. As you look at the produce section, do you recognize a number of the plants we've covered in this lecture? I think so; let's just kind of look at that imaginary produce section: You walk in, and what are you going to see? You're going to see cabbages, probably a couple different kinds; you're going to see plain old regular cabbage, you're probably going to see something called savoy cabbage, and if you're in a real gourmet store you might even see an orange-colored cabbage, they do exist. You're going to see the cauliflowers, and they may come in a variety of colors now. You're going to see kohlrabi, you're going to see kale, and you're going to see Brussels sprouts; all those things out of the Cole family.

You move a little bit further along and you'll see things from the Solanaceae. You're going to see tomatoes, probably a variety of different kinds. You're going to see potatoes, and not just one kind; there are going to be Yukon Golds, there are going to be russets, and there are going to be several different things. Again, if it's a fancy store you may see some purples ones and you may see some long kind of misformed looking things; there are lots and lots of new kinds of potatoes coming into this country. They're really old cultivars from Latin America, but they're coming in here now because people have interests in these kinds of interesting foods. Then you're going to see lots of legumes: You're going to see chickpeas, you're going to see snow peas, you're going to see green beans, you're going to see common peas, you might see some fava beans; you can see all that sort of stuff. The produce section is going to be heavily influenced by a number of things in this oligarchy of the garden patch that we just talked about.

But is that where you're going to end up seeing the plants? If you were talking about these plants and the grains, I think not. Let's move into the center of the aisles and start looking at some of the labels. First of all, let's go into the breakfast cereal aisle. That's no big surprise; what's in there? Grains; grains on top of grains on top of grains. Let's go into the snack aisle; what do we have in there? We have peanuts, we have potato chips, we have corn puffs; we have all kinds of things in bags with all kinds of flavor and stuff on them, but they're coming from 2, 3 kinds of plants by and large. Let's go over to the dairy case: You're going to look in there and you're going to see tofu in there, you're going to see something in a bottle that looks like milk, but it's going to be soy for people who have trouble with milk proteins; you can now get something that tastes, acts, and functions like milk but it's made out of soy protein.

You're going to go over to where you have some canned things and some bottles of stuff and what are you going to see? You're going to see pickles that are cucurbits, you're going to see all sorts of stuff like sauerkraut, and you might even see some kimchee; so that stuff is all in this relatively small group. You can say, "Alright, I'm tired of all that, I'm just going to go over to the soft drink aisle; that'll take care of it, I'll just go over to the soft drink aisle." You go over there and, of course, you have rows and rows and rows of carbonated soft drinks, and all of them that aren't made with aspartame or some of the diet stuff are going to be sweetened with corn sweeteners. So you run over to the refrigerated section and you start looking at the prepared foods, and if you start reading the labels: corn sweetener, corn sweetener, corn sweetener, corn sweetener. Of course, you go to the shortenings and there's going to be canola oil and all that sort of stuff. It's a small number of plants processed different ways, prepared different ways, and packaged different ways giving, if you will, almost the illusion of great variety. Our diet is not as varied as we think it is, and this is an important, and to many, a surprising fact. We will return to this point in later lectures.

In the next lecture, we'll discuss food preservation and storage, paying particular attention to plants that are easily and effectively stored. This was of great importance before the development of modern food preserving techniques such as canning, freezing, and freeze-drying. Our food choices were even more limited in the days before modern food preservation and transport made it possible to enjoy a varied diet year round by being able to enjoy foods out of season. We'll see you then.

Lecture Nine
The Importance of Storage Crops

Scope:

Before the development of modern food-preservation techniques, the typical diet in the fallow seasons could be tedious, if not unhealthful. Hence, much attention was devoted to the development and cultivation of storage crops. Technology-based methods of food preservation and storage developed in the temperate regions have made it possible for people throughout the world to enjoy "endless summer" at the dinner table. This in turn has relegated some once-common storage crops to the list of heirloom varieties.

Outline

I. Before the development of canning, mechanical refrigeration, and freezing, plants that could be kept over fallow seasons were of great value.

II. Many storage crops are roots, so it was common for most households to have a "root cellar": a cool, dark place where storage crops could be kept.

III. In a root cellar, one could commonly find potatoes, sweet potatoes, cabbages, kohlrabi, rutabaga, turnips, carrots, beets, and parsnips, along with some specialized storage crops that have long disappeared from common use.

IV. As an alternative to the root cellar, some farmers planted crops like turnips and beets.

    A. These plants produce stems and leaves that can be eaten by people or grazed by animals during the growing season.

    B. They also produce large, underground storage organs that can be left in the ground well after the growing season is over. These can be harvested by humans or rutted up by animals as needed.

V. Fruits, with the exception of apples, posed a special problem when it came to storage. Most fruits are relatively fragile and quite prone to spoilage. Thus, the only way to enjoy fruit long after the harvest was to produce secondary products.

VI. The production of secondary products was a low-tech way of enjoying some of the benefits of fruits and vegetables in the fallow season.

    A. Drying has long been used to preserve fruits, some vegetables, and some meats. By as early as 4000 years ago, the ancient Egyptians were regularly drying a variety of fruits.

    B. Some menus still exist from Roman feasts and celebrations. Raisins were prominently featured in many of them, suggesting that Romans considered them a delicacy.

    C. Europeans have long been extending the shelf life of fruits by making "preserves," a collective term for jams, jellies, and marmalades.

    D. Fermentation can also yield secondary products with extended shelf lives. Fruit juices are sometimes fermented to ciders, and cabbages can be fermented to sauerkraut or kimchi.

    E. Pickling in salt brine is another low-tech way to make secondary products of a variety of plant materials.

VII. All of these low-tech preservation methods were in regular use long before the discovery of the microbial world in the 17th century and the later development of the germ theory of disease and spoilage.

VIII. The production of secondary products, whether by osmolarity or pH, is quite effective at inhibiting spoilage caused by bacteria.

IX. The use of spices in preserving food is an ancient practice.

X. In 1809, Emperor Napoleon Bonaparte awarded a prize of 12,000 francs to Nicolas Appert for his "wonderful invention." Appert's great achievement was based on sealing food in airtight jars that he then subjected to a boiling water bath.

    A. It was from that invention that the practice of food canning began. Whole industries sprang up, canning vegetables, seafood, meat, and condensed soups and stews.

    B. Canning can also be done at home with minimal equipment, making the technique available to a large number of people in a variety of circumstances.

XI. It has been known for millennia that cold retards food spoilage. There are accounts of ice being transported long distances into warm climates as early as the 11th century.

XII. For centuries, it was common practice for the people of northern Europe to take advantage of low temperatures in the winter to preserve food by freezing.

XIII. New, higher-tech methods of food preservation—canning, freezing, freezing with desiccation, vacuum sealing, and others—are able to preserve food in appealing condition indefinitely.

    A. We still use a number of products that were first preserved by the old, low-tech methods. Preserves, pickles, cured meats, and fermented food products are still popular though they are no longer essential as preservation techniques.

    B. Yet some food plants that were once popular, if not nearly essential, are now relegated to heirloom status or have disappeared altogether, victims to the advance of technology.

Suggested Reading:

Creasy, *The Edible Heirloom Garden*, 1–57.

Questions to Consider:

1. Beans and grains can be stored for months, so why does special care have to be taken with other plant foods?

2. Before the contributions of Appert and Birdseye to food preservation, what was grown in a typical kitchen garden was quite different from what is grown there today. Why do you think this is the case?

3. How many different methods of preservation of plant foods can you think of that do not involve canning or quick freezing?

4. Can you name some plants that were once common but have become quite rare as a result of modern preservation methods?

Lecture Nine—Transcript
The Importance of Storage Crops

Hello and welcome back. Because vegetables and fruits grow only in the warm season in the temperate zones, and because many of them don't store well, diets could be composed primarily of meat, dairy products, and dried beans and grains. Hence, much attention was devoted to the development and cultivation of "storage crops" that could be utilized throughout the fallow season until new crops of vegetables and fruits could be grown. Storage crops and some "low-tech" preservation techniques—for example, things like drying, salting, and others—helped make the temperate regions an environment where both science and technology could flourish; people could be well-nourished in those fallow seasons and they could work indoors on issues having to do with science and technology. Consequently, new technology-based methods of food preservation and food storage developed in those very temperate regions, and they've made it possible for people throughout the world to enjoy what we might consider an endless summer at the dinner table. This, in turn, has fed back and relegated some once-common storage crops to the list of heirloom varieties.

Before the development of canning, mechanical refrigeration, and freezing, plants that could be kept over fallow seasons were of great value. But let me put this, if I can, in historical context. Up until just about now, we have been talking about things that were prehistoric—the origins of agriculture, the spread of agriculture, the domestication of plants—you'll notice now that we have begun to move into an era where there are indeed written records and where we do have more information. That won't stop me entirely from periodically reaching back into prehistory to find the foundations of things, but this course, as we indicated in the opening lecture, is moving essentially in a chronological direction from the ancient past toward the present; and we've now moved to where we will have written records about many of the things that we will discuss.

We move, for example, to the Colonial period in the United States; we can find records at locations such as Mount Vernon, the home of George Washington, and Monticello, the home of Thomas Jefferson that make it very clear that their kitchen gardens—the kitchen gardens of that time—were heavily slanted toward the production of crops that could be stored and used during the winter. That's quite different than what we see in gardens today. Without such crops, food during the fallow season would have consisted of almost exclusively meat, dairy products, dried beans, and grains.

Many storage crops—but, of course, not all of them—are roots; thus it was common for most households at that time to have a root cellar. This is a cool, dark place where storage crops could be kept; and that's certainly not an ancient idea. I personally have had a lot of experience with root cellars; I know how they feel, how they look, and how they smell. In a root cellar one could commonly find potatoes (they smell earthy), sweet potatoes, cabbages (have a sort of botanical smell), kohlrabi, rutabaga, turnips, carrots, beets, and parsnips—some people probably don't even know what parsnips are anymore—along with some specialized storage crops that have altogether disappeared from common use. One might also find a barrel of apples stored somewhere in the corner of a root cellar from the late fall just after the apples were harvested, till late winter or early spring because apples would store that well, and they did provide a sort of pungent smell to the whole place.

As an alternative to the root cellar, some farmers planted crops such as turnips or beets. These are very interesting plants because they produce stems and leaves that can be eaten by people or grazed by animals during the growing season. Turnip greens, beet tops; these are things that still occasionally show up on menus. But these plants also produce large, underground storage organs that can be left in the ground well after the growing season is over. Then, these can either be harvested by human beings (dug up), or they can be rooted up by animals as needed; so here's another way of storing plant material well into the fallow season.

Fruits, with the exception of apples (which we just talked about), posed a special problem when it came to storage. Most fruits—think about a fruit, like a peach—are relatively fragile and quite prone to spoilage. Thus, the only way to enjoy fruit long after the harvest was to produce something called a secondary product. We talked a little bit about secondary products in the last lecture when we mentioned cabbage and kimchi; we'll talk now about secondary products. The production of secondary products was a low-tech way of preserving some of the benefits of fruits and vegetables in that long fallow season. Drying has long been used to preserve fruits, some vegetables, and even some meats.

Let's step back now in time, away from Colonial America, and go back to as early a time as 4000 years ago: It's known that the ancient Egyptians at that time were regularly drying a variety of fruits. They dried figs, dates, grapes, and possibly even plums to make prunes; so they were making raisins, dried figs, dried dates, and maybe prunes. The initial purpose of this practice—this practice of drying these fruits—was likely preservation, but the Egyptians, I think, quickly learned that this process that was to preserve these fruits altered the texture, altered the sweetness, and changed the flavor of the fruit, often in a beneficial way, turning that ordinary fruit into a kind of special delicacy. We also have some menus from Roman feasts, celebrations, and banquets; we actually have the written records of these telling what the people ate and saying what was ordered for the feasts and what was presented. In many of these, raisins, either by themselves or as a component of some other prepared entree, were often prominently featured, suggesting that the Romans considered them a delicacy that they were proud to serve to their guests.

In Europe, Europeans have long been extending the useful life of fruits by making what we have generally come to call "preserves"; that's a collective term for jams, jellies, and marmalades. In each of these cases, the secondary product is produced by boiling fruit or fruit juice with sugar that is added from the outside almost to the point of saturation. That'll end up giving you preserves; it'll give you jam or marmalade if you put some of the solid fruit back in, and in the case of the jelly you do that same sort of thing but you add a gelatinizing agent, usually derived from an animal source, to give you a slightly different secondary product. All of these things preserve the benefits of the fruit long after the growing season.

Fermentation can also yield secondary products with extended useful shelf life. Fruit juices are sometimes fermented into ciders, and, of course, cabbages can be fermented to sauerkraut or kimchi as we mentioned last time. I suppose we want to make the point wine is, in a sense, fermented grape juice; though I don't think wine was generally made as a preservative but was used for other purposes. Pickling in salt brine is also a useful low-tech way to make secondary products of a variety of plant materials for purpose of preservation but also taste enhancement.

All of the low-tech preservation methods just described were in regular use before the discovery of the microbial world by Anthony von Leuwenhoek in the 17th century, and then the later development of the germ theory of disease and I'm going to add spoilage; the germ theory of disease and spoilage. It's worth noting that Pasteur— Louis Pasteur, who played a role in the germ theory of disease—first became involved in microbes when he was asked to study problems with wine going bad. He was a person, even though we think of him in terms of his contributions to medicine, he was very interested in food and food preservation issues. He got into that by worrying about, if you will, "sick" wine—wine that went bad—and also we know that pasteurization, a heating process named for him, of course is used not to permanently preserve but to extend the shelf life of a number of foods.

Yet each of the secondary product forming practices just covered in effect do one thing: They inhibit the growth and metabolism of bacteria that cause food spoilage. Drying, that we talked about, or desiccation does what? It concentrates natural sugars and other metabolites that increase the osmotic pressure within the dried item beyond the point that can be tolerated by spoilage bacteria. Let me take a second now and just explain what I mean by that, because we're going to go back to osmotic pressure several times. Think about a bacterial cell: It's a tiny little cell with its insides surrounded by a very fragile semi-permeable membrane. That means some things can pass through the membrane, some things cannot, it is semi-permeable. Water also can pass through the membrane. The membrane separates the inside of the cell from the outside of the cell, but both the inside and the outside are aqueous—both are essentially water environments—with lots of materials dissolved and suspended in them. Water can move back and forth across this membrane; some of the dissolved materials can and some can't.

When you add high concentrations of sugar or high concentrations of salt, they essentially don't pass through the membrane easily; they sit outside the cell, and what do they do? They tend to draw water out of the bacterial cell into the environment of the outside. That causes the cell to shrivel and ultimately die or at least grow very, very poorly. These bacterial cells don't have all of the equipment of more advanced cells that can pump things and whatnot, and so they're quite susceptible to this. The process can run in the opposite direction, too, where pressure can cause water to go into the cell, but most of these microbial cells have a wonderful, tough integument on the outside; a kind of outside barrier that works like the hull of a submarine and keeps them from imploding from the inside. Osmotic pressure is a way to control bacterial growth, and it's used in pickling and making of preserves. Dissolved salt can raise the osmotic pressure, and if sugar is added, that also can add to the osmotic pressure and help preserve food.

Fermentation of foodstuffs by a group of bacteria called the *Lactobacilli* and some other useful bacteria tends to lower the pH in the secondary product below the point of tolerance for the spoilage bacteria; again, we're going after those spoilage bacteria. Please note that in the production of secondary products, whether by osmolarity or pH, it's effective at inhibiting the spoilage caused by bacteria. However, I think almost all of us have experienced something with these secondary products, and we are familiar with them, and that is that occasionally we'll find a mold growing on the surface of something that's dried, pickled, or preserved. That's because there are a number of aerobic mold spores in the air, so they can easily affect these things; and many of these molds are quite tolerant to high osmotic pressures and low pHs. People have been dealing with this problem in a very pragmatic way for as long as these preservation practices have been in use. What do they do? They simply scrape off the mold and throw it away. Since most of such contaminants—these mold contaminants—are obligate aerobes, they don't penetrate the product more than a millimeter or 2, and mechanically removing them often restores the product to its useful state. Again, if you do see a mold growing on top of your marmalade, don't be too upset; you can simply scrape it off and taste it carefully, but you can probably continue to use it.

The use of spices in preserving food is, of course, a very ancient practice. It's long been known that peppercorns and cloves condition food products in such a way as to preserve their shelf life. It very likely was for their preservative value every bit as much as for their gustatory enhancement that these plant materials were so avidly sought. We also know, and you can prove this in the laboratory, garlic has some antibacterial activity, and thus also can provide some level of assistance in preserving foods. But you can actually do the experiment: You can take a petri plate, put bacteria on it, you can put down a piece of garlic, you can put down a clove, you can put down a peppercorn; all of these substances will give you a little zone of inhibition of bacterial growth. Peppercorns and cloves are substantially more effective at that than garlic, but all 3 work to some degree.

Thus, some meats are preserved with a combination of salt for osmotic protection, spices and garlic for their antibacterial activity, and then that treatment is finally enhanced by a process called "smoking," which essentially amounts to long, slow cooking that kills some spoilage bacteria without undue drying or cooking of the meat. Things like salamis and bolognas can be done in that way and they're going to have longer shelf lives than fresh meat. In fact, some of you may be aware of a product that you can buy in the meat market that has an old American name: It was called "summer sausage." The reason for that was that you could make the sausage in the winter when it was cold, and then without refrigeration that sausage would be edible throughout the summer because there was enough garlic, pepper, spices, salt, and it had been smoked. So these low-tech methods could make a difference.

Now let's move forward a little bit in time to 1809, and the Napoleonic Era. The Emperor Napoleon Bonaparte once awarded a prize of 12,000 francs to a man named Nicolas Appert for his "wonderful invention." What was Appert's great achievement; what did he do that was worth 12,000 francs to Napoleon? What did he do that makes him worthy of a place in history? It seems so simple to us today, but it was truly revolutionary: Appert took glass jars that he could seal tightly—he could make them airtight—and he stuffed them with food, added a little water to fill them up, and then sealed them tight. Then he took this little item—this sealed up glass bottle, airtight, containing a food item and a little bit of water—plopped it into a boiling water bath, and he did some testing. He left these objects in for different lengths of time, and he tested for 2 things: One, he tested for how long the food would be preserved; what its shelf life before he detected any spoiling? Two, what was the condition of the food? Here you have 2 opposing issues, don't you? If you want to extend the shelf life of the food, boil it longer; but if you want to have food that more closely resembles the fresh food that you put in there in the first place, you want to boil it a little bit less. In the Appert method, it was a kind of balancing effect to get the optimum: good shelf life, something that might last maybe a year or more, but that also clearly resembled the food that was put in there in the first place.

Remember, Napoleon was not only a great strategist, he was a master of logistics; he knew how to get material to the front, and he knew how to keep his army in reasonably good shape so that it could march and fight better than other armies. So this master of logistics quickly appreciated the utility of Appert's invention that allowed him to supply his armies with much higher quality food than his adversaries were able to give their men; you remember he said something to the effect that armies travel on their stomachs.

It was from that invention that the practice of food canning began. Whole industries sprang up preserving by canning items such as vegetables, seafood, meat, and then later in the United States, condensed soups and stews. These became huge, huge industries, and they became American household names, these concentrated soup companies, various canned food companies. Certain parts of the United States experienced great benefit; places where certain seafood could be harvested around the Chesapeake Bay and down into Delaware, big canning industries developed. That really did create an economic boost to the United States; and did allow some of these unique food items that could previously only be experienced by the people who lived around where they grew because they spoiled quickly and couldn't be transported at that time, now these things through technology could be canned and shipped around the world.

There's another interesting aspect to canning: It can also be done at home with a minimum of equipment—remember Appert didn't have a lot of equipment—thus making the technique available to a large number of people in a variety of circumstances. Home canning can be a big deal. I think, as we see people becoming more interested in returning to the soil, growing their own food, being interested in what's in their food, maybe even worrying about their economic situation, I think we're going to see more people engaged in home canning. That's both good and bad: I'm delighted that people want to grow their own food; I'm delighted that they want that level of independence. But canning at the level of the industry depends a great deal on very good science and very good microbiology. The vast number of people who can things have no problem, but remember some of the dangerous pathogens in food are both anaerobic (they don't require air), they can be somewhat acid-tolerant, and they're somewhat heat resistant. So when you go to the family picnic and Aunt Sally gives you her cold 3 bean salad and stands back and proudly says, "I grew these beans myself and canned them myself," think twice. If Aunt Sally hands you her cooked green beans, don't be too worried; because once you take these things out of their canning jar and heat them up, that's then plenty good enough and you'll be alright. But diseases like botulism do pop up around home canning experiences.

It's been known for millennia that cold retards food spoilage. There are accounts of ice being transported long distances into warm climates as early as the 11th century, and the practice probably is older than that. For centuries, people in temperate climates have used icehouses, springhouses, and ice boxes to try to keep water in a frozen state so that it could be used to retard spoilage and help preserve food; or, heaven forbid, in some cases preserve corpses until appropriate steps could be taken. The ready availability of mechanical refrigeration devices suitable for home use began in the developed countries sometime between the First and Second World Wars of the 20th century. It was common practice for centuries for the people in northern Europe to take advantage of freezing temperatures in the winter to preserve food by freezing. However, the texture, taste, appearance, and aroma of foods preserved that way often changed substantially between the time the item was committed to the cold and when it was ultimately used and consumed.

By 1916, an American, Clarence Birdseye, began his efforts to produce frozen fish that would rival fresh-caught fish for appearance, flavor, aroma, and texture. It turns out that Birdseye did a little stint as a fur trapper in the Northern Canada, and while doing that, he made the observation that some people who caught fish up there and very, very quickly froze the fish by simply pitching it into a very cold pile of ice, when that fish was fished out later or taken out later and prepared it clearly resembled the fresh-caught fish. What Birdseye figured out was that quick freezing made a big difference, and he began to devote his life to the development of quick freezing techniques, which me now know do much less damage to the cell structure of fish or other food items that are being frozen. Quick freezing is the deal; not slow freezing which allows ice crystals to form inside cells then ruptures cells and causes the material to be kind of mushy, get a bad texture, and opens the door to bacterial spoilage at some later point.

He also—and this may not sound like a big deal, but it turned out it really was—greatly improved the wrapping and packaging practices having to do with storing frozen foods, and that allowed them to be handled and used much better. He finally began his own company in

1924, and by all accounts, all of his products were really quite outstanding.

Now let's think about something: Let's think about how technology takes over when a new idea comes in. Birdseye was making really good frozen food products, but transportation of frozen items was still a problem. You could freeze the stuff in his plant; if you had to throw it in the back of a lorry or a railroad car that wasn't refrigerated, it would melt, it would be ruined. Then, where would it go? Most retail stores at that time did not have significant space for frozen items. Finally, even if they did, most households in the developed countries didn't really have adequate places to store frozen foods, even though they were acquiring mechanical refrigerators; so even if they went to the store and bought the frozen food, if they didn't use it immediately, what could they do with it? It was a sort of technological "chicken and egg" problem: What comes first? The supermarkets expanding their capacities, the industry expanding their capacities, the homeowners expanding their capacities, marketing to get people interested in these things? It's a long story, but we now know the outcome: Hard work and perseverance by a number of people in the retailing industry, the manufacturing industry began to produce a kind of new industry that allowed frozen foods to play a very important role in the lives of people in developed countries, and the frozen food industry was off to the races.

The new, higher-tech methods of food preservation—canning, freezing, freezing with desiccation (or what is called freeze drying), vacuum sealing, and combinations of these things and others—are now able to preserve food in appealing condition virtually indefinitely. Yet even in the face of that, we still encounter and use a number of products that were first preserved by the old, low-tech methods. Preserves, pickles, cured meats, and fermented food products are still popular, though they now are no longer essential as preservation techniques. Instead, they stand as examples of our learned food preferences that often hearken back to an earlier time when technology was less advanced. Yet at the same time, we must appreciate that some food plants that were once popular, if not nearly essential, are now relegated to heirloom status or have disappeared altogether, victims of the advance of technology.

In our next lecture, we'll deal with 3 of our most common, useful, and, I must say, beloved domesticates: dogs, cats, and chickens. These 3 early domesticates played very important roles in our transition to the process of food production and they helped lay the foundation for the advent of civilization. I'll look forward to seeing you then.

Lecture Ten
Three of Man's Best Friends

Scope:

This lecture deals with 3 of man's oldest, most important, and most cherished domestic animal partners: the dog, the cat, and the chicken. Dogs have been partnering with humans since well before the Neolithic Revolution and likely accompanied us on our journey out of Africa to settle the other major land masses. Chickens and cats have been domesticated for at least 9000 to 10,000 years and have been familiar, abundant, and useful partners to us along the path to civilization.

Outline

I. Dogs are undoubtedly humans' first animal domesticate. Domestic dogs arose from wild wolf populations.

   A. There is archaeological evidence dating back well before the Neolithic Revolution for the existence of domestic dogs, but recent genetic studies suggest that the first domestic dogs may have arisen as long as 35,000 years ago.

   B. Dogs may have contributed significantly to their own domestication. It is thought that a variant of the wolf population with a reduced flight response for humans may have carved out a niche around human garbage dumps.

II. Anyone who spends time with "house cats" knows that the word "domestication" does not fit these animals quite as well as it does dogs.

   A. There is evidence to suggest that cats and people cohabited as long as 9000 years ago. Cats buried with people of high status suggest a special relationship between the 2 species.

   B. Recent genetic studies suggest that all modern domestic cats arose from a single type of wild cat in the Middle East, likely from a single domestication event.

   C. Storage of harvested and planted material attracted small rodents. With the influx of rodents came an influx of cats.

III. It was about 4000 years ago in ancient Egypt that the breeding of domestic casts for special traits began. The Egyptians, as grain farmers, saw the utility of the cat. Their admiration of feline qualities also lead them to deify cats.

IV. Sailors, like farmers, were plagued by rodent pests; cats thus became commonplace on ships and boats. As a result, the domestic cat spread rather quickly around much of the globe via human sailing and trade routes.

V. Modern cat breeders and cat fanciers have stretched and molded this small feline into a wide variety of shapes, sizes, colors, and coat types.

VI. The third animal is not as adorable as a dog or cat, but the number of domesticated chickens on the planet and their distribution across the human landscape suggest that humans and the chicken have formed a most successful partnership.

    A. Chickens are the most widely distributed and numerous birds on the planet.

    B. The frequent reference to chickens in everyday expressions like "nest egg" and "pecking order" also bespeaks a close relationship.

    C. There is agreement that chickens arose primarily from red jungle fowl. This furtive bird lives in an extended territory throughout Southeast Asia.

    D. There is good evidence that chickens were being domesticated in Asia at least 10,000 years ago and were widespread among the global human population by at least 3000 years ago.

VII. Chickens were probably rather easy to domesticate and to alter by selective breeding.

    A. Hens can lay several eggs per week, and a hen that is broody will incubate the eggs of other hens as well as her own.

    B. The gestation period in the egg is only 21 days, so a number of hatches can be accomplished in one season.

    C. Chickens tend to stay close to where they were hatched and raised, returning to roost each evening.

VIII. Originally, most chicken breeds were dual purpose, producing both meat and eggs. In recent times, selective breeding has been used to produce "broilers" and "layers."

Suggested Reading:

Clutton-Brock, *Domesticated Animals from Early Times*, chaps. 3, 10.

Dohner, *The Encyclopedia of Historic and Endangered Livestock*, chap. 8.

Questions to Consider:

1. What other uses are found for chickens, beyond meat, eggs, and entertainment?

2. What is there about chickens that made them particularly well suited for being rapidly spread around the globe?

3. Why are viral chicken diseases much more feared and problematic today than they were in the past?

4. What were some of the traits displayed by early dogs that made them attractive partners for our Paleolithic forebears?

5. Why do you suppose that dogs appear to have accompanied our early ancestors in their initial journeys of exploration and colonization as they spread across the globe, while cats seem to have radiated out to established human populations at a later date?

Lecture Ten—Transcript
Three of Man's Best Friends

This lecture deals with 3 of man's oldest, most cherished, and important domestic animal partners: the dog, the cat, and the chicken. What do I mean by domestication? Let's go back and talk about that again. There are really a number of characteristics: First of all, there is a kind of codependence that should exist between human beings and the domesticate; the domesticate should depend on the human being, and the human being should be able to depend to a degree on the domesticate. There should be a distinct genetic impact: The domesticate should be genetically distinct from its wild progenitors; you should be able to tell the difference genetically. Domesticates need to be something that's kept by people. That's different from a pet; a human being can keep an animal as a pet and not have it be a domesticate, because it may not be genetically different from the wild type. There be no codependence; but that's a requirement for being a domesticate: it should be kept by people at some point. Then, finally, there should be benefit; and I made a point early on that if this really is working well, it should be a mutual benefit: benefit to the domesticate, benefit to the human partner. These traits can be applied to a different degree, and can mean different things, to different animals.

Let's talk first about dogs. Dogs have been partnering with man since before the Neolithic Revolution, before we became food producers; and dogs likely accompanied our ancient ancestors as they journeyed out of Africa to colonize and ultimately settle on all of the major land masses save Antarctica. Chickens and cats have been domesticated for at least 9 to 10 thousand years, and they've been familiar, abundant, and useful partners to us along our path to civilization.

Dogs are undoubtedly man's first animal domesticate; it's also clear that domestic dogs arose from wild wolf populations. There's archaeological evidence based on bones and teeth dating back well before the Neolithic Revolution for the existence of domestic dogs, but recent genetic studies involving mitochondrial genetics that we discussed earlier suggest that the first domestic dogs may have arisen as long as 35,000 years ago. That goes back well before we were food producers, and does talk about the time when man was beginning to colonize regions outside of sub-Saharan Africa. Dogs have contributed significantly to their own domestication; remember we talked about that before: domesticates often meet us at least halfway. It's thought that a variant of the wolf population with reduced flight response for human beings may have begun to carve out a niche around human garbage and refuse dumps.

Let's stop for a second here and think about that: We talked earlier about the fact that all wild populations have a range of genetic variants. Flight response is an important survival characteristic, but there probably were some genetic variants within the wild wolf population that became more tolerant of man, were not as afraid of him; they probably also were drawn to that garbage and to that refuse. There's another point: This creature, which we can start to call "protodog," probably wasn't as large as some of the other wolves, may not have been as ferocious and may have been sort of ostracized to the edge of the wolf population, maybe didn't find a appropriate mates and things, but found refuge around these refuse heaps. Man also sometimes fought off potential predators that could have also been predators for this protodog. This creature, protodog, probably began to develop its own habitat close to human beings, and probably didn't provide an significant competition for human beings; and so not only did it tolerate people, but people tolerated it.

Over time, then, men began to apply artificial selection techniques to these creatures, producing the large array of dog types that helped our early ancestors enter and colonize this variety of habitats. We made one reference to that some time ago when we talked about the Inuit peoples who moved into very cold, icy habitats and probably could not have done that had they not been accompanied by their dogs. Archaeological evidence suggests that dogs accompanied, then, these Paleolithic ancestors as they moved into and colonized these significant land masses.

Today's dogs can play a huge number of roles for human beings; they remain very close to use: They can be sentries, they can give us warning; they can guard our property and our person; they can herd other animals; they can be great assists in hunting and retrieving hunted animals; they can trail creatures, like Bloodhounds do; they can be draft animals, they can pull things for us; and they are effective military and police assistants. A growing number of dogs are now being used as human assistants, the best-known of which are the so-called "seeing eye dogs," but dogs can do many things to help people. They're also starting to be used a bit in medicine because their very keen senses may help them detect certain diseases if they can be trained appropriately; and, of course, they can be beloved and useful companions to many of us. It's their keen sense of hearing and smell, and their visual acuity in dim light, areas where we're not very good as animals. We don't hear particularly well, we don't smell well at all compared to other animals, and dim light is a problem for us. We see well in bright light, maybe better than a dog; and dogs have a different structure to their retina and they see very well in dim light. Those things taken together have helped us as their partner, if you will, extend our sensory probes into the world around us; something terribly important to prehistoric man moving into new environments.

Dogs also bring one other interesting trait with them when they leave the wolf world: Wolves howl; and they do it fairly rarely and for specific purposes. Dogs bark. We still don't know what dogs are saying when they bark; I think they're just saying, "I'm here, I'm here, I'm here," or, "You're there, you're there," but the point is barking dogs can be very useful because they are working as sentries. With their better seeing, their better hearing, their better smelling, and their ability to bark they extend our sense out far beyond what they would be without them; it makes them a very useful partner.

Attendance at a dog show illustrates the vast array of sizes and types in the canine world. However, it must be remembered that these creatures are all members of the same species and what we are seeing is the impact of years of artificial selective breeding to give us all these different types with their different functions and eye appeal. What do we mean by selective breeding? It's a rather simplistic technique. Let's say we're doing something as simple as trying to get a bigger dog. I have several different dogs breeding; I look at this group of puppies and I take the biggest one, he's a boy, and I go over to the other set of breeding dogs and I take the biggest girl I can find, and I put them together and let them have puppies, and in the next generation I look for the biggest one again. I keep doing this and surprise, at the end you're going to get a Mastiff, a Great Dane, an Irish Wolfhound, something very big. That's the way selective breeding works. It's also based on culling—or not allowing to breed—other animals that you're not particularly interested in. It's selecting the types you want to get the properties you want.

If breeding restrictions were completely relaxed in the dog world and you simply let dogs interbreed across these various types, it wouldn't be too long before we would essentially reestablish something that probably looked a little bit like protodog. It would probably be about 60 pounds; it would have a sturdy brown or brown-black coat; and it wouldn't show really any of these peculiar characteristics that we see in some of our specialized breeds like Pugs, Bulldogs, or Afghans.

I should point out again that dog habitat is very much like our own. I'll just toss in a little story that I experienced a few years ago when I was in Nicaragua. I was visiting a family that I'd been helping do something, and they were very short of food and they had very little in the way of physical resources. When I went in their modest home, there were the children playing on the floor, and asleep in the middle of the floor was a dog, admittedly skinny and not particularly well-kept. I asked through a translator, "Is that your dog?" The question wasn't really understood, so I modified it; I said, "Do you feed that dog?" That actually got a laugh through the translator, because these people had trouble feeding themselves, they certainly weren't going to feed the dog. I was puzzled, and I said, "Why is the dog here?" I got a very straightforward answer: "This is where he lives." It really underscored this issue of overlapping habitats and tolerance with each other and minimum competition. Dogs live where we do, and that's an important thing to keep in mind.

Anyone who spends time with housecats, as I do, knows that the word "domestication" doesn't fit this animal quite as well as it does dogs; we talked about that earlier. There is evidence to suggest that cats and people have been together for a long time; we've probably cohabited for at least 9000 years. We know that cats were buried with people of high status back about that time, which suggests a special relationship between the 2 species. But were these early cats domesticated, or just tamed and tolerated, or admired small cats of which there are many types? Again, we have to return to that same question: the difference between an animal that is simply tamed and tolerated, or one that is domesticated. I'm going to make the case that cats are domesticated, because I'm going to use some of those characteristics we've talked about before: I think they are genetically different; I think there is a degree of codependence, or at least there used to be a significant degree of codependence. Certainly, human beings do keep cats; and so we can make the case that domestication is probably a word that we can apply to our feline friends.

©2009 The Teaching Company.

We think that these animals—in fact, there's now good evidence—arose in the Middle East from a domestication event that began to separate them from a small type of wild cat that lived in the region. What we mean by a domestication event is the beginnings of a move to genetically alter the animal and make it different from its wild progenitors; and simultaneously, as a result of that, bring it into contact with human beings who begin to keep it, live with it, to gain some benefit from it, and the cat also beginning to gain some benefit as well.

Cats are obligate carnivores, and that's a very important thing to note. They also have exceptional gifts as hunters of small rodents and even some snakes; and if you've ever had the pleasure of watching a cat hunt you'll realize how wonderfully acute its hearing is, how keen its eyesight is, but once it spots its prey that's when you get the real excitement. This is kinetic energy ready to explode, and then you see an array of weapons that are really quite astounding. When a cat—which can look very sweet—opens its mouth and yawns, you'll see very large canine teeth or fangs, you'll see some bone crushing teeth in the back, and then you'll see the other powerful weapon, the retractable claw. Cats can be very silent, they can move with their claws retracted, but when they pop those claws out they have a dangerous, sharp weapon and they are extremely good with their feet. They can catch a bird in flight with one paw—I've seen that done—and they can jump and twist and they're just extremely good at hunting. Remember: They are obligate carnivores.

When human beings made that great transition that we keep talking about during the Neolithic from being food procurers to becoming food producers, one of the technical problems those early farmers ran into was how do we store our grain and our seeds? How do we store our seed stock and our grain? The grain, of course, had to be dried and stored to be used when it wasn't available on the plants; that's one of the reasons grain was important. Also, these people needed seed stock; from the beginning, they were saving seeds and replanting them, which help in that domestication of plants issue that we keep talking about. These people developed storage places that we would generally call "granaries"; places where you put grain. The minute you do that in an environment where agriculture began, you begin to attract small rodents. Small rodents have very high metabolic rates, and they will consume surprisingly large amounts of grain given their relatively small size. It is no small problem to have rats, mice, and squirrels in your granary if you're counting on keeping that grain for human use. The cat was drawn to its potential prey, the small rodents, and the cat was very effective at demolishing the population of small rodents in a fixed environment like a granary. Hence, our early agricultural ancestors began to appreciate the benefits that these cats could bring because not only were they terrifically good hunters who really knocked down the pest population, they were obligate carnivores, and they could care less about stored grain and seed stock; they didn't need it, so they were the ideal sentry. They would take out the invaders, protect the assets, but they wouldn't touch the assets themselves.

We know that it was in ancient Egypt that the breeding of domestic casts for special traits began about 4000 years ago. The Egyptians, as grain farmers, certainly saw the utility of the cat, and this story we just talked about—about cats being guardians—certainly was going on in Egypt, but probably without selective breeding until about 4000 years ago. The Egyptians' admiration of feline qualities literally led to them to deify of cats. As you know, cats show up in the pantheon of Egyptian gods; they were much appreciated by the Egyptians. Sailors, much like farmers, were also plagued by rodent pests. You had to carry bread, grain, or stores onto a boat, and keeping rats and mice off your boat was tough; but you could bring a cat on board, and the cat did just what it did with the granaries: put a hit on the rodents, didn't bother your stores. Then there was one other advantage: Cats don't particularly like to swim; they can, but they don't like water much. Once they found a nice home on a boat, they tended to want to stay there, even when the boat was at rest in a harbor. Cats quickly were dispersed around much of the agricultural area by trade and travel along sailing routes and trade routes because they were really working for sailors on their boats and on their ships.

Modern cat breeders and cat fanciers—and that's a word we're going to introduce several times in this course: the idea of a "fancier," someone who is just interested in or in love with a particular animal and is very interested in special types, and is interested in going to shows and maybe even competing with their animal against somebody else's animal for some particular trait; this activity is called a "fancy" and the people who engage in it are called "fanciers"—have stretched, molded, and manipulated this small feline into a wide variety of shapes, sizes, colors, and coat types; and you can look at pictures of cats or you can go to a cat show and you'll be astonished at how many different kinds of cat types we have and how these animals breed true, how they, in fact, do constitute real breeds. This is done through selective breeding, and this subject of making a breed and then maintaining it will be a subject of a subsequent lecture in this course.

But there's something else we need to go about both cats and dogs as it relates to this issue of genetic difference from the wild type. Certainly domestic dogs look different than wolves; certainly house cats, and cats in the cat fancy, look different from the wild cats from which they arose; but the reproductive isolating barriers between these domesticates and their wild progenitors are not complete. Genes can flow back and forth, and these animals can breed with wild types. In the cat fancy, we have some people breeding housecats that came from this domestication event in the ancient prehistoric Middle East and they're breeding them back to wild cats to make new breeds of things called, for one example, something called the Savannah Cat. These things are as large as a mid-sized dog, they're 50 or 60 pounds; and they almost look like an exotic animal, but they have emotional and behavioral properties quite similar to a house cat. That's an interesting situation. The same is true, by the way, with dogs: They went through the protodog stage, we clearly have our domesticated dogs, we have our breeds of dogs; but dogs can still breed with wolves, and there is a population of creatures out there called wolf dogs. Some people wanted to keep them as pets; not a good idea. People have been hurt by wolf dogs; they begin to revert back to being non-domesticated, which makes them more unpredictable.

There is no end of humorous stories about the differences in behavior between dogs and cats. While dogs tend to be loyal, subordinate, tractable, and capable of "unqualified love," cats tend to be aloof, standoffish, and sometimes rather independent. These traits derive from their lives as wild animals. Dogs originally were, and still are, pack animals that live in a communal group and recognize an alpha male and an alpha female. When a human being is able to usurp the role of the alpha, the subordinate, loving, and tractable characteristics of a dog immediately become apparent. Cats, on the other hand, arose from solitary hunters, and though they appreciate the food, shelter, warmth, and attention we sometimes lavish on them, they never really consider us to be "up to their standards"; as they say: Dogs have masters, cats have staff.

One measure of the degree of domestication of any animal is the degree of dependency it develops for human beings; that was one of our points to make an animal a domesticate. Though dogs are capable of reverting to a feral state and have and can form packs that have some capacity to fend for themselves, it's generally the case that without the support of a human partner, a dog would soon be in considerable distress. Cats, on the other hand, can quickly become feral and survive very nicely without any input from human beings, thank you very much.

The third of the animals I wish to cover today might surprise you. It happens to be an animal I care a great deal about; but not everyone, I realize, shares my enthusiasm for this animal. This third animal that we're going to cover is, admittedly, not as "adorable" in many circumstances as either a dog or a cat, unless, of course, you happen to be really hungry or if you're trying to "scratch out"—pardon the really bad pun—a living in a difficult and underdeveloped environment. The number of domesticated chickens on the planet, and the distribution of those birds across the human landscape, suggests that man and the chicken have formed a most successful "partnership." Estimates on the world-wide chicken population do vary widely, but I'm not kidding about this number: There have been claims made for as many as 24 billion of these birds in existence at any one time today. Chickens are undoubtedly the most widely distributed and the most numerous bird on the planet. Clearly, domestication was a good strategy from their perspective.

We know that linguistics has played a role in our ability to understand the relationship of human beings to domesticates, and we talked about historical comparative linguistics and we talked about following the spread of agriculture into new areas. One of the things that linguists look at is the frequency of use of words related to a particular subject, and that can be some measure of how important that subject is or how familiar that subject is. Just look at what happens in common speech that bespeaks the close relationship we have with chickens; just in English, the number of words that have a chicken basis suggests how close this relationship has been for thousands of years. Everybody is familiar with terms like "nest egg," "pecking order," "protective as a mother hen," "mad as a wet hen," "broody behavior," "running around like a chicken with his head cut off," "cocky," "cocksure," "cock of the walk," "cocktail," "strutting like a rooster," "scratching out a living," and many others that I'm sure you can think of.

There's good agreement that chickens arose primarily from a creature called the Red Junglefowl, and that furtive bird lives in an extended territory throughout Southeast Asia. It does look quite a bit like a domestic chicken, but, again chickens are genetically different, they clearly have a different kind of orientation to human beings— they are not particularly frightened by human beings; they operate nicely around us—and so they are distinct, they have been useful to us, we do develop a kind of co-dependence. There aren't very many feral chickens running around, if we don't take care of them they tend to be gone; so they do fit very nicely into our definition for a domesticate. We know that these creatures were domesticated from the Red Junglefowl about 10,000 years ago in Asia, but there's also data suggesting that these useful creatures were widespread in the global human population—and I mean global—by at recent time as 3000 years ago; so they quickly spread out in the human population after their point of domestication in Asia.

Chickens were probably rather easy to domesticate and to alter by selective breeding. Remember we talked about selective breeding with dogs where you keep the type that you want and you begin to stretch the makeup of the genetics of an animal to give you the type that you want. Chickens are fairly easy to deal with that way for a number of reasons; their biology plays right into that. Hens can lay several eggs per week, and a hen that is broody will incubate eggs of other hens as well as her own. After the hatch, however, the mother hen will take care of all the chicks until they're relatively independent. Hens not only protect their chicks, they are rather good teachers. I really never tire of watching my hens demonstrate scratching techniques to their peeps; and they don't just scratch and let the peeps watch, they poke them and get their attention and say, "Look; look what I'm doing," and they really do teach. The gestation period in the egg is only 21 days, so a number of hatches can be accomplished in one season. Chickens tend to stay close to where they were hatched and raised; they return to their roost in the evening; they're rather poor flyers; so, again, they tend to stay close to us, they don't go out and mix with wild populations, and they don't travel very far from their home. Again, that helps them fit that definition of a domesticate.

Originally, most chicken breeds were dual purpose—that is, they produced both meat and eggs—but in recent selective breeding associated with industrial use of chickens, the types have been broken into 2 general proprietary groups. There are "veal chickens" or "broilers" that are raised for very fast growth and they give you large amounts of very tender meat because the animals are very young when they are sacrificed; and then there are "layers," who may have very little flesh, but they produce a prodigious amount of eggs in their relatively short lifetime before they're recycled into dog food or wherever they go.

There are additional uses for chickens: They will do things like turn your compost pile; they will pick pests off your other animals; they even have some guarding capabilities, they'll make noise when an intruder comes in. I'm very pleased, always, to have chickens on my farm. They do bring a kind of joy to me that's not entirely different than some other people get when they interact with their dogs or their cats. When I'm having a really bad day, nothing perks me up better than walking out into the chicken pen carrying some feed and seeing these creatures run toward me with their odd gait, with their wings at their sides, and their sort of swaying stride as they come running toward me acting like they've just experienced the second coming.

Next time, we're going to move on to another group of barnyard creatures that also were domesticated early and have played an important role for thousands of years in our march from hunting and gathering to the establishment of civilization. We'll see you then.

Lecture Eleven
The Common Barnyard Domesticates

Scope:

In this lecture, we discuss the domestication of barnyard animals that played particularly important roles in the establishment of the food-producing lifeway. We look at sheep, goats, pigs, equines, and bovines. We also look at some aspects of the management and use of the modern descendents of these early domesticates. We conclude by asking, Could civilization as we know it survive without the presence of the animals and plants covered in this and the 3 preceding lectures?

Outline

I. Sheep domestication was probably limited to regions where wild sheep were plentiful and played some role as a prey species. There is evidence based on archaeological remains that domestic sheep arose from the wild Armenian mouflon between 8700 and 8200 years ago in the Fertile Crescent.

II. Goats, unlike sheep, are browsing animals and naturally occupy habitats that are rockier and more shrub covered. Examination of goat bones found in a number of archaeological sites suggests that modern domestic goats arose from wild Persian bezoar goats between 8700 and 8000 years ago in the eastern third of the Fertile Crescent.

III. Sheep and goats are quite compatible with each other and can be grazed and herded together. However, their different feeding habits have resulted in rather different behavior patterns.

IV. Pigs have been a good source of meat for humans for millennia. They are generalized, monogastric omnivores that can thrive on food scraps found near human settlements.

    A. They can also forage, root, and scavenge food from a variety of sources, so they are relatively easy to nourish.

    B. Wild pigs have a very broad range and thus may have been domesticated at a number of locations.

V. Horse evolution remains a complex story, with a number of dead-end species, a complex series of moves across the globe, and great extinction events.

   A. The first use made of horses was for meat, milk, hides, bone, and dung. It was only later that horses began to be prized for their motive power.

   B. The anatomy, physiology, and temperament of horses all factor into their domestication and their special place in human transportation and mobility in peace and war.

   C. All existing equines have some ability to interbreed with each other and produce offspring. In many cases, these offspring are sterile, but they are often larger, stronger, and more intelligent than either of their parents.

VI. There is some disagreement concerning the early domestication of cattle and other bovine species. Some suggest that there is evidence for their domestication as long as 10,000 years ago, while others set the time at about 5000 years ago.

   A. Whatever the actual date of domestication, it is generally agreed that cattle were domesticated after dogs, sheep, goats, and swine.

   B. It also seems clear that cattle were used first for meat, hides, bone, and horn.

   C. They were later used to provide labor.

   D. Finally, milking became an intense activity, with bovine milk providing a substantial portion of the nutrition of a number of cultures.

VII. Though there are several species in the bovine subfamily, we will limit our discussion to the water buffalo and cattle (members of the *Bos* genus).

   A. Domestic water buffalo are of 2 general types: the swamp buffalo of Southeast Asia and the river buffalo, probably best known to Europeans and Americans for its contribution of milk and the cheese derived from that milk.

   B. Domestic cattle, *Bos taurus*, evolved from the wild aurochs, *Bos primigenius*.

VIII. The milk of these animals, and that of other domesticates, can be consumed directly by humans, providing a nutritious addition to the diet. Secondary products, with different properties and longer shelf lives, have been in use in various cultures for millennia.

    A. Yogurt is a naturally occurring product of raw milk, which generally contains enough lactic acid bacteria to initiate the process.

    B. Like so many other food products, cheese was probably first developed in the Middle East. The practice of cheese making is thought to be about 4000 years old.

    C. Cheese can be made from virtually any kind of milk, and there are a number of ways to form and process curds once they are formed. As a consequence, there are over 400 distinct types of cheese.

    D. Butter is generally made from cow's milk. When whole milk or cream is churned, an emulsion of milk fats, air, and water forms this smooth, semisolid material that is prized in many cuisines.

    E. A by-product of butter making, buttermilk, is also useful in cooking or can be consumed directly.

Suggested Reading:

Anthony, *The Horse, the Wheel and Language.*

Dohner, *The Encyclopedia of Historic and Endangered Livestock.*

Questions to Consider:

1. Cattle, despite their obvious utility and great popularity, are thought to have been domesticated later than sheep, goats, pigs, and poultry. What is a likely reason for that?

2. Sheep and goats are often found on poorer pasture than horses. Why should these animals be better able to cope on poor forage than horses?

3. Knowing what you do about the nature of wild horses, provide a reason why researchers are entertaining the hypothesis that the 3 major branches of the family tree of domestic horses represent maternal lines started by 3 females all being bred to the same male?

4. The dentition of domestic pigs superficially resembles that of human beings. Why do you think that is the case?

5. If you can, try to develop an argument about why differences in food preference have resulted in significant behavioral differences between sheep and goats.

Lecture Eleven—Transcript
The Common Barnyard Domesticates

In the last lecture, we looked at some of the first animal domesticates. If you recall, at the beginning of the course, I made the claim that civilization couldn't have occurred without the domestication of plants and animals. I hope that you now have a better understanding of how, among other things, dogs enabled us to live safely in groups, cats enabled us to store grain and stop foraging, and chickens gave us both eggs and meat so we could reduce our need to hunt. In other words, early man was beginning to identify the characteristics of domesticates that would be useable in their efforts to settle, expand, and grow.

In this lecture, we'll again step back into the prehistoric to discuss the domestication of some important "barnyard" animals that played particularly important roles in the establishment of the food-production lifeway. We'll look at sheep, goats, pigs, equines (horses and horse-like animals), and bovines (cattle). We'll also look at some aspects of the management and use of the modern descendents of these early domesticates. There will be a brief discussion of the milking of some of these animals and a few of the secondary products derived from the milk so obtained. We'll conclude by asking the question: Could civilization as we know it survive without the presence of the animals and plants covered in this and the 3 preceding lectures?

Sheep domestication was probably limited to regions where wild sheep were plentiful and played some role as a prey species; that is, a prey species for us, meaning we hunted them. Sheep are grazing animals and do well in a steppe or in grasslands. There is evidence based on archaeological remains that domestic sheep arose from the wild Armenian mouflon between about 8700 and 8200 years ago in the Fertile Crescent, making it one of the first of these "barnyard animals" brought under domestication. The mouflon, that wild progenitor of the domestic sheep, once roamed much of the Eastern Mediterranean basin, but today is found in the wild today only on isolated mountain tops in the Eastern Mediterranean islands of Corsica and Sardinia. Several years ago, I traveled to the mountains of those 2 islands and spent considerable time hiking and looking for examples of that reclusive animal. They do exist in zoos, but they're pretty hard to see in the wild. I was fortunate enough to finally see a male with a small "harem," a small group of females, and a few young.

What I discovered, of course, is that the mouflon are dark brown animals, and the male has very large curving horns. Knowing what I do about the changes that often attend domestication, I was not particularly surprised to find that these animals were larger than domestic sheep, they were more fleet of foot—they could really fly through the scrub—and they were extremely agile. Also, it was clear that they were much more fearful of the presence of man, exhibiting a strong flight response. Given that the mouflon is all but extinct in the wild today and there are billions and billions of sheep in the world, we have another example of domestication appearing to be a good "choice" or "strategy" for the domesticates as well as the domesticator.

Goats, unlike sheep, are browsing animals and they naturally occupy habitats that are rockier and more shrub-covered. Examination of goat bones found in a number of archaeological sites suggest that modern domestic goats arose from wild Persian bezoar goats between 8700 and 8000 years ago in the eastern third of the Fertile Crescent. Because sheep and goats are reasonably easy to herd, these creatures spread across and ultimately outside the Fertile Crescent fairly soon after their initial domestication. Sheep and goats are quite compatible with each other and can be grazed and herded together. However, their different feeding habits have resulted in rather different behavior patterns if one cares to actually observe closely. Sheep are as grazers, and they spend a great deal of the time with their heads down looking at forage; they're looking for what to eat, they're looking at the ground. They do have a sense of curiosity and can show interest in their surroundings, but those tendencies to be curious and to look around are not really strongly developed in these animals. They do, however, have a strong flocking tendency and quickly clump together at the first sign of any trouble or danger. They're not very adventurous and they're thus rather easy to confine so long as they have the company of other sheep. A single sheep is a very unhappy animal.

Goats, on the other hand, as browsers, generally have their heads up looking for new twigs or branches to browse. They're willing to eat tough weeds and shrubs as well as pasture, so they can be very useful to farmers in clearing new land for farming. Unlike sheep, they're very curious and show considerable interest in all aspects of their surroundings. They'll stay together when being herded, but they don't have the same flocking drive that sheep display. They can be quite difficult to confine, unlike sheep, and are known as real escape artists as they try to seek out new browsing areas. Recently, on a trip to the Pyrenees, I had the privilege of following a flock of several thousand sheep ewes that was being moved from the wintering areas to summer pastures. There were a number of goats tagging along with this flock. When I tried to get the shepherds to tell me why, they alluded to the fact that it was good to have the goats because they were smarter than the sheep and helped move the flock along. They also, as an aside, pointed out that they tasted pretty good, as well.

Both of these species are ruminants, possessing a multi-chambered stomach including a rumen which is in essence a large fermentation chamber containing numerous cellulose-digesting microorganisms. The presence of this rumen permits both sheep and goats to prosper on fairly low-quality browse or forage. We'll return to the importance of this to our theme in a few moments.

Pigs have been a great source of meat for humans for millennia. They're generalized, monogastric omnivores that can thrive on the food scraps found near human settlements. What we mean by generalized monogastric omnivore? It means that they can eat a wide range of food types. They have a dentition that'll allow them to eat meat, it'll allow them to eat grain, it'll allow them to be scavengers; but what they eat goes to a single stomach, as is the case with us. They can forage, they can root, and they can scavenge food from a variety of sources, so they're really relatively easy to nourish. They're also highly fecund, producing fairly large litters on at least an annual basis—and if managed intently, you might get them to breed a little bit more often than that—giving these early breeders ample opportunity for selective breeding opportunities and to practice artificial selection; to go for the types and forms that they liked the best, that performed the best.

Wild pigs have a very broad range and thus may have been domesticated at a number of different sites. There is evidence for domestication in the north-central region of the Fertile Crescent from the Eurasian wild boar, an animal that lives wild in that area, and they can show that it happened between 8500 and 7000 years ago. But there are also claims made for an even earlier domestication in

China. Domestic pigs are generally smaller than their wild progenitors and they reach sexual maturity earlier causing juvenile traits to persevere into adulthood. This characteristic, called "neoteny," is not unusual in domesticated animals. It's even true, for example, in dogs: If you look at the traits of an adult wolf and you look at the traits of a wolf pup, you'll notice that adult dogs, if they haven't been modified too much—for example, to become brachiocephalic, or have one of those pushed-in faces that Bulldogs have—you can see that there's a little bit of the immature wolf preserved in the mature dog; this is neoteny. The size of the tusks in the males are also generally smaller—another neotenous trait—than in wild pigs; that's a trait that makes domestic pigs much easier to be around than wild boars, though care still has to be taken when dealing with pigs because both sexes, the males and the females, can and do bite. Every year we hear about some person who's engaged in raising pigs being attacked by one of these animals and they are sometimes killed and pretty badly mangled. Pigs have to be dealt with carefully.

Since pigs are not easily herded, they tended to become isolated in little islands or pockets in a number of defined locations around specific human settlements, giving rise eventually to a very rich variety of forms and types that are the foundation for the many modern breeds that we have. Of note for this course, they also provided a ready supply of meat that could be kept penned, didn't need to be taken out to herd, and required less land to maintain. So here again, this helps make civilization possible in multiple environments and circumstances through the various traits of given domesticates.

Horse evolution still remains a complex story with a number of dead end species and a complex series of moves across the face of the globe and several great extinction events. The story may have begun in what is now North America, but at just about the time of the arrival of the first modern humans on that continent, evidence for the existence of horses disappeared from the Americas. It's thought that the modern domestic horse arose on the steppes of Eurasia, probably descended from a recently extinct animal known as the Tarpan—I've only seen pictures of Tarpans, they're extinct; they look horse-like, but they have distinct differences from modern horses—though the story of the provenance of the domestic horse is hardly settled, with a number of different theories still under consideration; this is an active area of research, and people are, I think, zeroing in on the question very effectively. I think in a few years we're going to know pretty much how the domestic horse came into being.

The presence of multiple mitochondrial DNA types in domestic horses suggests one of 2 things: There were either multiple domestication events happening probably in close proximity but in different places and at different times; or there is another possibility. This is the one that I favor: What you have is 3 different maternal lines arising from the breeding of 3 different mares probably to one confined wild stallion. Why do I favor that one? If you've ever been around wild stallions, you realize how difficult these animals would be to capture and to handle, and then how difficult they would be to get into a breeding situation that wouldn't damage either them or the mare. This may be a situation where some early domesticators found possibly a smaller, slightly more docile, less flight-oriented stallion and captured him. Once they had him, they then put him with probably more than 3 mares but ultimately got 3 successful maternal lines going. No proof of that; but my tendencies are to favor that hypothesis based on what I know about wild horses and horses in general.

The wild progenitors of horses were probably a declining group—not like we see with sheep or goats where they're flourishing in a particular area—limited in distribution to the Eurasian steppe. It's likely that this was not a place where these animals were doing terribly well, but rather may have been a sort of last refuge. Remember equines were going extinct in various ways and at various times around the globe; but because they were in that sort of refuge place and became domesticated, that may have very much contributed to their survival. What we have here is yet another example of the benefits of the partnership between animals and humans; a benefit to the humans, but very possibly also a significant benefit to the animal.

The first use that people made of horses after their domesticators was probably for meat, milk, hides, bone, and even dung, which was used as a fuel. In fact, horse droppings when dried make a very nice fuel because horses don't process their manure quite the same way that the ruminants do. It was only later that horses began to be prized for their motive power, both to do work and to carry people either on their backs or by pulling wagons, chariots, or some other conveyance. The anatomy, physiology, and temperament of horses all factor into their domestication and their special place in human transportation and mobility in peace and war. Horses are monogastric herbivores; that's one of the reasons that their dung, when dried, makes a pretty good fuel. They do best on high-quality forage and they like some grain in their diet. Some have described the modern horse as an actual "running machine"—I realize that's kind of a homely term—but it may be an apt description. Even the heavy-boned draft horses are relatively fleet of foot when compared to other "barnyard animals."

Horses have a very large nasal airway—they have to bring a lot of air into their lungs in order to support their activity as a running animal—but they can't breathe through their mouths. Their plumbing up around their head is different than our own; when we get out of breath, we open our mouths and breathe through our mouth. A horse doesn't get any benefit from having its mouth open, all its air comes in through its nose. This has permitted horsemen over the years to successfully fit an implement called a bit into the mouths of horses, permitting them to be controlled—because you can pull their head around way one or another—without impeding their ability to draw in large amounts of air to support their muscular activity while they're running. Horses often when they're harnessed up to be used have a bit in their mouth; if you'll notice, some other animals don't have that when they're harnessed up, they have a yoke or something else, and they don't have anything inserted into their mouth.

We know that all existing equines have some limited ability to interbreed with each other and produce offspring. In many cases, these offspring are sterile and incapable of reproducing, but these sterile offspring are often larger, stronger, and more intelligent than either of their parents. Mules are the result of crossing a horse with an ass or a donkey. These animals have great utility as beasts of burden. The art and science of mule-making may have reached its absolute zenith with, again, Napoleon Bonaparte, that master of logistics. He developed a gigantic mule by using the big French draft horse, the Percheron, and crossing it with the world's largest asinine species, the world's largest donkey, which is still today found in France and a few of those animals are now in the United States, and I've had the pleasure of looking at them; they're quite interesting to observe.

There's some disagreement concerning the early domestication of cattle and other bovine species. Some suggest that there is evidence for domestication of these creatures as long as 10,000 years ago, while others set the time only to about 5000 years before the present. We're pretty relaxed about time in this prehistoric era, but 5000 years? There has to be a reason. Part of the uncertainty comes from the fact that before cattle were confined, their herds were followed by pastoralist peoples who later herded these cattle, but still did not routinely confine the cattle. Confinement and more intense artificial selection probably did not begin until some of these "semi-domesticated cattle" became small enough and comfortable enough with humans to permit confinement and genetic manipulation. I think that situation accounts for that sort of 5000-year uncertainty.

A few things seem do certain about the process of the domestication of bovines, however. It's certainly agreed that whatever the actual date of domestication, cattle were domesticated after dogs, sheep, goats, and swine. It also seems clear that cattle were used first for meat, hides, bone, and horn. Later, these beasts were used to provide labor, and they could produce significant power when hitched to a plow or something of that sort. Finally, milking became an intense activity, with bovine milk providing substantial portions of the nutrition of a number of cultures.

All bovines are ruminants, like sheep and goats, so they have the capacity to gain a significant portion of their nutrition from cellulose. What difference has this made in developing civilization? Sheep, goats, and cattle can live on very low-quality forage or browse, and civilization based on those domesticates was sustainable even in harsh environments. These animals are very good at converting low-quality forages into meat, milk, or other products. So, as noted earlier, multiple varieties of domesticates enabled civilization to rise around the world in a range of circumstances. We can see, now, the utility of these various animals and plants as early civilizations began to take root.

Though there are several species in the bovine subfamily, we'll limit our discussion to the water buffalo and cattle, members of the genus *Bos*. Water buffalo have been domesticated for at least 4000 years. Domestic water buffalo are of 2 general types: The swamp buffalo of Southeast Asia is generally used as a draft animal, aiding in the cultivation of paddy rice. The river buffalo can also be a draft animal, but is probably best known to Europeans and Americans for its contributions of milk and the cheeses derived from that milk. True mozzarella and ricotta cheeses should be made from buffalo milk, not the more easily-obtained cow's milk. Despite this iconic role of the water buffalo in modern Italian culture in *cucina*, it should be noted that the dictator, Benito Mussolini, made an effort to eliminate the water buffalo from Italy because he felt it linked Italians to more "primitive" cultures; amazing.

Domestic cattle, *Bos taurus*, evolved from the wild aurochs, *Bos primigenius*. The now-extinct aurochs were grouped into 3 populations that evolved separately over time. European-type or taurine cattle, do not have those big humps on their necks or backs and are thought to have been derived from one of those strains of aurochs; while zebu, or humped cattle, were likely derived in a separate domestication from one of the other aurochs strains that had evolved separately over the years. In addition to being without a hump, taurine cattle do not have a set of muscles under the skin that allows them to twitch their skin as zebu do; this means taurines can be bothered more by flies because they lack one of the mechanisms for repelling flies that zebu have. DNA studies suggest that the sanga cattle of Africa are the result of yet another domestication, but one that involves input from both taurine and zebu strains.

The practice of removing the young from a lactating cow after she's had a calf, or a ewe after she's had a lamb, or a nanny after she's had a kid for the purpose of milking that animal and extending the lactation period came after cattle, sheep, and goats were domesticated for other purposes. This does a couple of things: It creates small, immature animals that can go as meat sources for things like baby lamb, kid, or veal. It also means that you can extend the lactation period of the mother by milking her on a daily, or multiple times daily, period, and you keep the milk coming and you can use it for a number of sources. The milk of these animals, and that of other domesticates, can be consumed directly by humans providing a nutritious addition to the diet, but secondary products with different properties and longer shelf life, or longer useful life, have been in use in various cultures for millennia.

Yogurt is a naturally occurring product of raw whole milk, which generally contains enough lactic acid bacteria—members of the genus *Lactobacillus*—to initiate the process of yogurt-making. It should be noted that if you go to the grocery store and pick up a bottle of milk and want to make yogurt from it you have to go through some other steps, because your milk's been pasteurized, many of those lactic acid bacteria have been killed, and if you just set that milk out it won't turn to yogurt, it'll spoil, because there are some spoilage bacteria left in there. Spoiled or sour milk is not yogurt; yogurt is a very different product made by the activities of these *Lactobacilli*. It was probably first developed in the Middle East or Asia Minor, but it was known to be serving as a portable, nutritious food source for the Viking raiders by the time they were pillaging and sacking costal Europe in the 8th through the 12th centuries. So yogurt gets all the way up into Scandinavia, and we know that Scandinavians today still like their yogurt; but it also was probably centered originally in the Middle East, and the fact that the *Lactobacillus* that makes yogurt is called *Lactobacillus bulgaricus* suggest that there may be a fair amount of yogurt eaten in Bulgaria as well.

Like so many other food products, cheese was probably first developed in the Middle East. The practice of cheese making, though, is thought to only be about 4000 years old. We talked in an earlier lecture about how secondary products from plants expand their uses, and we see the same case here with cheese and yogurt, not to mention the many other secondary products that can be derived from animals. Cheese can be made from virtually any kind of milk, and there are a number of ways to form and process the curds once they're formed. Remember cheese is essentially a collection of the solid materials from milk, the curd; the liquid, or whey, is usually discarded in the cheese making process. There are over 400 distinct types of cheese known and within each of those types there are a number of variants; so cheese is a wonderfully rich, cultural expression of what we can do in the making of a secondary product from something like milk.

Butter, of course, is generally made from cow's milk. When whole milk or cream is churned an emulsion of milk fats and water form this sort of semi-solid that's prized in many cultures for cooking or for using directly; and, of course, a byproduct of butter making is buttermilk which can also be used.

We've talked about some of the most successful domesticates, but there were many failed efforts as well. We know that many attempts were made to domesticate creatures and they just did not work out. We've now focused on a relatively small number of domesticated animals, and I would like to leave you with the question now: Where would the civilized world be had we not been able to successfully domesticate these organisms? I've tried to make the case all along that civilization could not have come about had it not been for the domestication of some of these key animals; I hope by now that point has been amply made. But another way to examine the same question would be: Where would civilization be if we simply pulled away all of our domesticated plants and animals? Let's say just the ones we've talked about so far: the cereal grains, the few plants we've talked about that make up much of the bulk of what we eat, the products provided to us by these animals we've talked about, and the services we've received by dogs and cats. I think the case is made that civilization is dependent upon these domesticates.

In the next lecture, we'll go into greater depth in discussion of the methods plant and animal breeders employ to "improve" the breeds and varieties that they have, and then conserve the fruits of their labors in true-breeding, predictable genetic packages. We'll see you next time.

Lecture Twelve
Landraces, Breeds, and Strains

Scope:

In this lecture, we look at the systematic effort of plant and animal breeders, stockmen, and horticulturists to group and organize the organisms they wish to employ. We discuss the systems used to place similar organisms into useful groupings and the methods employed to make sense of and optimize the rich heritage of domesticated plant and animal genetic material that has come down to us from those first prehistoric peoples who began the practice of domestication.

Outline

I.   From this point onward, we will confine our discussions to the past few hundred years and focus on events and activities that have a direct impact on the present and the future.

II. As livestock spread out from their points of origin, groups of animals became essentially permanent residents in some localities. If no efforts were made to intervene through selective breeding, considerable heterogeneity in unselected traits usually accumulated. Such a naturally occurring, localized collection of animals is called a landrace.

   A. Both natural selection and artificial selection can play a role in formation of a landrace.

   B. If no effort is made to control variability within a landrace by inbreeding, considerable variation can accumulate in traits outside those controlled by strong selective pressures in the prevailing environment.

III. We do not have written records as to when deliberate breeding began, but it is safe to say that some few hundred years ago, efforts became more consistent. As herdsmen and breeders began to more closely observe and regulate populations, the first steps to the establishment of standard breeds began.

   A. The first steps involve developing a list of standard traits that will be selected for or against: the breed characteristics.

B. Stud books or compilations of pedigrees need to be developed and kept.

C. Comparisons of animals at shows or fairs allowed multiple breeders to see and discuss breed characteristics and hopefully come to agreement on them.

D. In time, animals with agreed-upon traits that tended to be passed on to their offspring when bred to the same type began to be referred to as breeds.

E. Through controlled breeding, breeders took steps to preserve desired characteristics and eliminate traits that were negative or generally frowned upon. As a consequence, artificial selection and controlled breeding began to trump natural selection.

F. A breed is a collection of genes that should result in an animal with a known and predictable set of characteristics defining the breed and should breed true for those traits. In order to breed true, a trait needs to be fixed.

IV. As understanding of genetics advanced, a subset of breeders began to pay as much or more attention to standards of beauty as to standards of practicality. In this way, I tend to think that a breed is a social, as well as a biological, entity.

V. From the forgoing, one might conclude that the only way to get to a standard breed is through a landrace. Though that is often the case, it is not an obligatory step.

VI. There is a strong pragmatic streak that runs through animal agriculturists. Landraces and standard breeds certainly have considerable utility, but other groupings could be imagined that would have great utility based on phenotype rather than on genetics.

VII. The lives of most people in the developed world are increasingly being impacted by proprietary industrial strains.

VIII. Though plant breeders tend to operate in much the same basic way as animal breeders, the differences in the reproductive systems of plants and animals lead to some practical divergence between the groups.

A. Record keeping is still essential. It is important to know which traits are being followed, and they must be accurately described or measured.

B. Controlled breeding is the driving force in selecting the desired strain or variety—and in keeping it predictable and more manageable, which is increasingly critical as our codependence continues to rise.

C. Plants can often self (be cloned). This gives the plant breeder several advantages over the animal breeder. It is inherently easier to maintain genetic continuity from generation to generation if sexual reproduction can be avoided.

D. Plants that make seeds or bulbs that can be stored for reasonably long periods without loosing viability provide another advantage to the plant breeder, who does not have to freeze sperm or embryos in liquid nitrogen as animal breeders often do.

IX. There are significant differences in the terminology used by plant and animal breeders. We never speak of breeds of tomatoes or wheat but rather talk about varieties or strains of plants within a given species.

X. It should be noted that plant and animal breeders had remarkable success in selecting useful traits and combining them into valuable collections of genes without having the slightest idea of how genetic systems actually operated.

Suggested Reading:

Sponenberg and Bixby, *Managing Breeds for a Secure Future*, chaps. 1–3.

Questions to Consider:

1. Texas longhorn cattle can come in a wide variety of coat colors. Why do you suppose that is the case?

2. What advantages accrue to herdsmen as a result of the development of breeds? Can you think of any disadvantages?

3. Why is it easier to maintain a plant variety in a constant genetic state than it is to maintain an animal breed in a genetic steady state?

Lecture Twelve—Transcript
Landraces, Breeds, and Strains

To now, we've seen how cats, dogs, chickens, sheep, goats, pigs, and horses helped humans to expand, settle, and acclimate to the formation of settled communities. Specific characteristics in these creatures made these partnerships initially helpful and then ultimately essential to the work of civilization. We could not allow this to happen solely by chance if we were going to survive; our codependency on these creatures required a certain degree of predictability.

In this lecture, we will look at the systematic effort of plant and animal breeders, stockmen, and horticulturists to group and organize the organisms they wish to employ in their work. We will look at the systems used to place similar organisms in useful groupings, and we will take a look at some of the methods employed to make sense of and optimize the rich heritage of domesticated plant and animal genetic material that has come down to us from those first prehistoric peoples who began the practice of domestication.

Though this course is intended to cover the interaction of human beings and their domesticates for the past 10,000 years, or the period when domestication of plants and animals set our species on the path to civilization, we've spent much of our effort thus far dealing with prehistory and the establishment of the agricultural way of food production. From this point onward, we will confine our discussions to the past few hundred years rather than the past 10 millennia and focus on events and activities that have direct impact on the present and likely even the future. A recurring theme in this course has been that natural selection helped prepare a number of what we've been calling "proto-domesticates," both plant and animal, for domestication. In every case, however, the practice of human-directed artificial selection, implemented by controlled breeding, actually finished the process. This lecture will be about the early and the ongoing efforts to refine that process.

Landraces may have come into being as the result of natural forces acting on plants or animals that human beings had already domesticated, but it has been only in the last few hundred years that we've seen humans make a determined effort to make sense of this phenomenon and derive practical benefits from it. As livestock spread out from their points of origin, groups of animals became essentially "permanent" residents, if you will, in some localities where local production requirements and physical conditions worked together to create new sets of conditions and selection pressures that resulted in a recognized type or form that could be reliably distinguished from other members of the same species. If no efforts were made to intervene through selective breeding, considerable heterogeneity in unselected traits could and usually did accumulate. Such a naturally occurring, localized or regional collection of animals is generally called a landrace. That's what we mean by a landrace: It's one of these sort of isolated little islands of animals, initially domesticated but then brought to a particular form or type by natural selection.

Both natural selection and artificial selection can play a role in formation of a landrace. Though landraces are sometimes referred to as "local breeds" or "natural breeds," I feel that terminology confuses the situation and detracts from the definition of the word "breed" that I plan to define shortly. If no effort is made to control variability within a landrace by intentional and purposeful inbreeding—that is, by breeding back to close relatives—then we can see considerable variation accumulate in all sorts of traits outside those controlled by strong selective pressures in the prevailing environment. By way of illustration of that point, it can be pointed out that in the landrace that gave rise to the Texas Longhorn there was really no selection pressure for coat color. Thus the landrace that preceded Texas Longhorns and the Texas Longhorns themselves have no uniform color standard and can show a wide range of colors and even coat patterns. Thus, it is common to find considerable heterogeneity for a number of unselected traits within any landrace.

Good examples can also be found among the Florida Cracker Horses, Florida Cracker Cattle, and Soay Sheep. The things that selected those landraces and kept them functional where they were are survival traits. Things like color can change, ear set can change, and all sorts of things like that; but it's the survivability traits that were selected for in those landraces. To illustrate that point, if you visit the Florida Cracker people and look at their horses and their cattle, if you look at them in profile they look rather normal; but if you look at them head-on they're very narrow compared to other horses or cattle. They're like the thins on a radiator; they're thin so they radiate out heat very effectively, and that makes their survivability much better in the hot, humid, muggy, swampy climates in which they live. That's selected for; the other traits aren't.

We don't have written records as to when deliberate breeding began, but it's safe to say that some few hundred years ago the efforts became more consistent, and as herdsmen and breeders began to more closely observe and regulate these populations, the first steps to the establishment of standard breeds began. We might wonder why this arose as a need. It's because the enterprises related to these animals gradually began to be more dependent upon these animal partners having specific characteristics as opposed to just the general usefulness as food or fiber. Remember the faster, smaller rabbits that we talked about in an earlier lecture that we used to illustrate the distribution of genetic types across a population and how natural selection could begin to pick out a different collection of genes to make that quicker, faster rabbit? As with the rabbits, the quest for cows with better milk production, horses with greater speed, and so forth led to efforts to breed for improved outcomes (improved defined by people). In other words, as civilizations flourished, new environmental pressures arose which demanded predictability.

The first steps in developing a standardized breed involve developing a list of standard traits that will be selected for or against; that is, the breed characteristics need to be developed. Secondly, stud books or compilations of pedigrees need to be developed and kept. On-site comparisons of animals such as occur at shows or fairs needed to be developed so that multiple breeders could see and discuss the breed characteristics themselves, and hopefully come to agreement on them. In time, animals with agreed-upon traits that tended to pass these traits on to their offspring when bred to the same type began to be referred to as standard breeds. At this point, breeders generally took steps through controlled breeding to preserve the desired characteristics and eliminate the traits that were negative or generally frowned upon. As a consequence, artificial selection and controlled breeding began to trump the natural selection that had helped create the landraces that had given rise to the breed.

A breed then, is a collection of genes that should result in an animal with a known and predictable set of characteristics defining the breed and it should breed true for those traits. In order to breed true, a trait needs to be "fixed." You'll recall that in our discussion of chromosomes we talked about an organism being homozygous (big word, homozygous) for a given gene if both copies of that gene—the one received from the mother and the one received from the father at the moment of conception—were both the same. In that case—in that homozygous case—when sex cells are made and those 2 genes separate into different sex cells, a [homozygous] individual can only contribute that form of the gene since that's the only form it has. That would not be true if the organism was [heterozygous] for that gene. Thus, to make a gene pair homozygous is to "fix" it since that organism can only provide that gene type in a mating.

As understanding of genetics advanced, a subset of breeders began to pay as much or more attention to traits that they wished to enhanced or eliminate. This led to controversy as they argued about the future direction and the genetic heritage of the animals they husbanded. In this way, I tend to think that a breed is a social, or if you will even a political, entity as well as a biological entity. A breed is defined by a set of inherited characteristics determined by the people who determine the breed standard, and not by nature. The finest specimen of any given breed may not have particularly good survivability in a natural setting; that is, in the wild. If you don't believe me, take a good look at a champion English Bulldog. Dogs like to breathe; those animals have been bred to have a face and a physiognomy that makes breathing very difficult. Some breeds have more to do with human amusement or interest than they do with any benefit to the animal; and I'll give you another dog example: Picture a Pug and I think you'll see what I mean.

Since breed standards are determined by people and people can disagree, it's usually necessary to develop some form of breed organization that develops widely agreed upon standards, mediates in disputes among breeders over those standards, and maintains the records and registrations for the breed. Such organizations also often organize shows or competitions to display the best of the breed to aficionados and to the general public, and to educate breeders about the best agreed-upon traits of the breed. Now do you see why I consider a breed a social or political as well as a biological entity? We might even wonder why we need to maintain these animals any longer, when the purpose they serve has become so personalized, but such is the state of our civilization that we can afford a partnership that is for pleasure as well as utility. Our predecessors would have been quite surprised, no doubt, at the pampered lives some animals now have. Nevertheless, that is part of our story of evolving domestication; and I certainly fall into that category of animal pamperers.

In order to maintain a breed in its pure form, specific steps need to be taken. There needs to be a registry of all animals that will take place in intra-breed mating; you have to have a registry. Only animals that meet the criteria of the breed and conform to the breed standard can be allowed to be registered. Also, in order to be registered, an animal must be the product of a mating between 2 other registered individuals; so this becomes a kind of a closed family, if you will. If care is not taken, excessive inbreeding occurs and some negative and unregulated traits can begin to accumulate. We can look at some examples. Look at dogs with hip dysplasia; let's look at some breeds of dogs with genetic blindness and tendencies toward cancer. Let's look at thoroughbred racehorses that are having catastrophic breakdowns on the racecourse. Think about dogs that are subject to things like bloat; think about difficulties in birthing in Holstein cattle. Can you think of a reason for why these problems would start to pop up? There is a reason for it: The really dangerous deleterious genes are usually recessive. It means when they are in a heterozygote, they're not expressed, but if they appear in homozygous form, trouble happens; the trait is expressed, cancer's produced, hip dysplasia happens, in the case of racehorses the skeleton isn't strong enough to stand up to the forces created by the muscles, and so on. Because these animals are closely related, their chances of matching up 2 of these recessive genes increase. That's one of the things we have to constantly be on guard for as we engage in inbreeding.

Despite major efforts to maintain a given form in a breed, breeds of animals do change over time. A glance at a Victorian portrait of a Great Dane will reveal a dog that looks quite different from the Great Dane champion you will see in the Westminster Dog Show on television. Why is that? It's because mammals have to reproduce by sexual reproduction; and what is sex for? Sex, we think, in biological terms exists not for reproduction but for the purpose of mixing genes. As mammals evolved and gave up asexual reproduction and were stuck with only sexual reproduction, it's very hard to freeze characteristics in time. Animal breeders are trying, and they may be able to fight against such change over time by relying more and more on frozen sperm and frozen embryos that they put down in liquid

©2009 The Teaching Company.

nitrogen baths; but again, this is a high-tech solution to a practical biological problem.

In the absence of controlled breeding, the population drifts toward the most fit—that's those quick rabbits again—rather than the most "desirable" type ("desirable" as defined by a human being). We can look at the characters from the popular film "Lady and the Tramp" and we can see that point. Those of you who've seen that film can picture Lady; she's the epitome of pulling the genes in the gene pool toward a particular type, and that type is preserved by only letting her consort with creatures that look like her. But her new friend, Tramp, just looks like a dog. Why? He's the product of lots and lots of matings that weren't controlled and he's the result of the gene pool drifting back toward the, if you will, protodog; he's going to have great survivability, he's going to be smart and strong and quick, but he's not going to be "pretty" and meet the standards that people set.

From the forgoing, one might conclude that the only way to get to a standard breed is through a landrace. Though that is often the case—for example, the Belgian Malinois dog came out of the landrace of Belgian sheepdogs before they were organized into a standard breed—it's not, however, an obligatory step. Breeders have been known to "construct" a whole new breed from known stock in an effort to improve some trait or group of traits. That would be the case with, for example, the Jack Russell Terrier (we know somebody put that animal together) or the Dishley Leister Sheep, which we're going to talk about at some length later in this course.

There's a strong pragmatic streak that runs through animal agriculturists. Landraces and standard breeds certainly have considerable utility as we've just said, but other groupings could be imagined that would have great utility based on phenotype; not the genotype, not the genetic makeup, but the actual form, function, and structure of the animal that you see or experience. A good example of such a "type breed"—and that's what we'll call one of those—would be the Pinto horse breed. Its characteristics include what you can see; it's a useful group. You look at the animal—you don't know anything about its parentage—you look at it and you say, "Ah, it's a Pinto," and you can put it with other Pintos and you can expect that it would do things. It's useful in that regard, but its genetics lack predictability in reproduction. The same characteristics in offspring can't be predicted with any great certainty; thus, it's really of very limited value as a genetic resource. That's a different situation, then, than a standard breed or even some landraces.

Increasingly, the lives of most people in the developed world—people like most of us—are being impacted by proprietary industrial strains. These groupings are not generally considered breeds because they are seldom shown or entered in competitions and rather than having their standards set by a breed organization, they are bred to meet an industrial standard for production and that standard can constitute proprietary information held by the company or corporation that bred them and intends to use them in a production system. This practice is common in the turkey, chicken, and swine industries of today.

Let's take a quick look at how the need for control and predictability with plants mirrored those of animals. Domesticated plants also represent a defined collection of genes that result in established and predictable phenotypes. Remember we talked about phenotypes as being the expression of the genes; the expression that you can see, measure, and so on. Though plant breeders tend to operate in much the same way as animal breeders when it comes to the basics, the differences in reproductive systems of some plants and animals lead to some practical divergence between these 2 groups.

When I say there's similarity in regard to the basics, what are some of those basics? Record keeping is still absolutely essential. It's important to know which traits are being followed; you have to describe that. You have to be able, in the case of plant breeding, to accurately describe or measure the traits that you're going to follow. Again, much like the practice followed by animal breeders, plant breeders use controlled breeding as the driving force in selecting the desired strain or variety they're after, and then keeping it predictable and more manageable, which is increasingly critical as our codependence continues to rise. This keeps us in that positive feedback loop we discussed earlier. Remember that positive feedback loop? We talked about more mouths to feed means you have to exert more control over nature to put more land in production, and you have to use that land more intensely and more effectively. That's exactly what we're talking about here. If we need more food, we only have 2 ways to get it: use more land, use it more effectively. What's one way to use it more effectively? Be able to use domesticated plants, in this case, that have absolutely predictable properties that you can manage to fit the circumstances to optimize the amount of food produced and help you stay at least a step ahead in that positive feedback loop continuing to provide adequate nutrition for an ever-expanding population.

That's what this is really all about; but stop and think about this again: Whether it's animals or whether it's plants, it has to do with this degree of intensity, it has to do with our codependency because we've now put our faith in these domesticates. We've allowed our population to grow to this size and we now absolutely depend on these plants and these animals providing what we predict they can provide, and we can't really leave that to chance. We have to be able to have breeds or cultivars that we know we can manage genetically, that we can predict their outputs, because too much is riding on pure chance. The plant breeders and the animal breeders are under the same kind of pressures to produce this kind of predictability and this kind of productivity.

Again, plant breeders do have some advantages over animal breeders. Plants can often "self," or they can be cloned. This gives plant breeders several very big advantages over animal breeders. Remember we said that animal breeders have a problem sort of freezing a breed in time? They tend to drift one way or another; the Great Dane has changed over time, and so on. We know that they're trying to come up with a technological solution to retard that change by freezing embryos and freezing sperm that they can pull out and keep reusing the established types before they drift off. But the problem is it's always dependent upon sex. In animals, every time you want a new generation—a new dog, a new sheep, a new cow— you have to put a male and a female together somehow, have sex, and the offspring, because it's sexual, is not going to be identical to either parent or to any of its siblings.

Not true with plants, because plants can easily be cloned. Many of us have experienced this. We think of cloning as a big high-tech thing; how many times have you seen someone go in somebody's house and say, "Gee, I love that vine. Look at the way it's growing, it's beautiful; I'd love to have that." Somebody says, "I'll give you a cutting," and they go over with the scissors, they cut some off, they stick it down in a glass of water; and in a couple days, roots are growing out, you take it home and stick it in a pot, and now you have the plant. It's genetically absolutely the same plant; the plant has been reproduced by making a clone. There's been no sex, no mixing of genes; you've had reproduction—you had a plant in this house; now you still have that plant and you have a plant in the other house, but no sex—it was done by cloning, asexual reproduction, and both plants are genetically identical to each other. Plant breeders can easily do that.

If they have a plant that doesn't clone easily and they have to reproduce sexually, some plants can "self." That means that they can pollinate their female organs themselves; they have both organs on the same plant. Though that is sex, and though the seeds that are likely to be produced many not produce a plant that's genetically identical to a parent, this is carrying the concept of inbreeding about as far as you can imagine. What closer relative can you think of to breed to than yourself? The only way you can match that in the animal world is with hermaphroditic animals, but most animals that are hermaphroditic are self-sterile—they can't fertilize themselves—and the few that can seem to be of almost no economic importance; so that's a whole area that's denied animal breeders.

Plants that make seeds or bulbs that can also be easily stored for reasonably long periods of time; so in a practical sense, you can also keep your material around and bring it back when you need it without having to put embryos or sperms down in a bath of liquid nitrogen as animal breeders often have to do. There are also significant differences in terminology employed by plant and animal breeders. We never speak of breeds of tomatoes or wheat, but rather talk about varieties or strains of plants within a given species.

It should be noted that plant and animals breeders had remarkable success in selecting useful traits and combining them into valuable collections of genes comprising landraces and breeds of various kinds without having even the slightest idea of how genetic systems actually operated. Their work was practical and pragmatic; it had huge impact—it's terribly important—but much of it was entirely empirical and was based on minimal or actually incorrect understanding of the processes actually at work. It was not until the middle of the 19th century that some obscure work in an unpretentious monastery garden began to provide the clues that lead, in time, to a revolution in genetic science. Later in this course, we're going to go to that garden.

Now that we have a good grasp of the concepts behind domesticated species, landraces, and standard and type breeds, let's explore ways in which some of these plants and animals, as well as some "interesting" microbes, became "world travelers" as a result of the activities and adventures of some of the major figures in the age of exploration. We'll look into that next time.

Timeline

Before Present (BP)

200,000–150,000........................Anatomically modern humans
(*Homo sapiens sapiens*) appear
in Africa.

100,000–35,000.........................*Homo sapiens sapiens* moves
into and occupies the rest of the
"Old World."

60,000–40,000...........................Micronesia and Australia are
colonized and occupied by *Homo
sapiens sapiens*.

40,000–11,000...........................*Homo sapiens sapiens* crosses the
then-dry Bering Straight to the
"New World."

35,000–14,000...........................The dog becomes *Homo sapiens
sapiens*'s first domesticated animal,
and the bottle gourd becomes the
first domesticated plant.

14,000–10,000...........................The end of the Paleolithic period;
From this time to the end of the
Neolithic period, stone tools become
more sophisticated.

c. 13,000....................................There is evidence for the cultivation
of rye in Syria.

c. 11,000....................................Monumental structures are built at
Gobekli Tepe in Turkey;
Domestication of sheep and goats
begins in the Middle East.

10,000–8000 ....The most recent ice age ends.
Agriculture begins (the Neolithic
Revolution), and human beings
begin to occupy fixed settlements in
various locations around the world.

c. 9000 ....Chilies are cultivated and
improved in the Americas;
Wheat is cultivated and
domesticated in the Middle East.

8000–3000 ....The mighty aurochs is gradually
converted to the domestic bovine
through selective breeding. The
domestication of chickens begins in
Southeast Asia, possibly from
multiple origins.

c. 7500 ....Rice begins to be domesticated
in China.

7000–6000 ....Grapes are under cultivation,
and alcoholic beverages are made
by fermentation.

7000–4000 ....Primitive forms of maize are
developed in Mexico.

c. 6500 ....Domestication of swine begins
in China.

c. 5500 ....The domestication of alpacas and
lamas begins in the Andes.

c. 5000 ....Evidence exists for the beginnings
of the Bronze Age; Sheep begin to
be bred for secondary products such
as wool.

c. 4500–4000 ....The domestication of horses begins.

c. 4000 ....Beets are cultivated and improved
in Europe.

c. 3800 ....Beginnings of rye domestication in
Southwest Asia.

c. 3100 ....There is evidence for the beginnings
of the Iron Age.

c. 3000 ....Oats are domesticated in central
Europe; Most Mesolithic cultures
are gone or in severe decline.

3000–2500..............................The first biblical writings appear.

c. 2000....................................Eggplant domestication occurs in the India-Burma region.

A.D.

800–1400................................Feudalism is the prevalent political and economic system in Europe.

950–1000................................Horseshoes, horse collars, and moldboard plows are developed in Europe, significantly increasing the food supply.

1300–1350..............................The Black Death sweeps through Europe, greatly reducing the population.

1492–1550..............................Christopher Columbus makes his first voyages to the New World, and the first stages of the Columbian exchange take place.

1671 ....The last sighting of a wild aurochs occurs in Poland.

1735 ....Carolus Linnaeus publishes *Species Plantarum*, providing a systematic approach to the study of plant species.

c. 1750....................................The early stages of the Industrial Revolution.

1760–1790..............................Robert Bakewell uses systematic breeding approaches to produce improved breeds of cattle, sheep, and horses.

1793 ....Eli Whitney invents the cotton gin, initiating the practice of applying the methods of the Industrial Revolution to agricultural production.

1798 ....Thomas Robert Malthus cogitates on and writes about the interdependence of population density and available resources.

1809 ....Nicolas Appert invents the process of canning, providing a new approach to the preservation of food.

1845–1851................................The Irish potato famine occurs due to destruction of a potato monoculture by a fungus.

1860s..Louis Pasteur, Robert Koch, and others propose and refine the germ theory of disease.

1865 ....Francis Galton publishes "The First Steps towards the Domestication of Animals."

1866 ....Gregor Mendel reports on his genetic experiments to the Natural History Society of Berlin.

1868 ....Charles Darwin publishes *The Variation of Animals and Plants under Domestication*.

1870–1895................................Luther Burbank develops the Burbank potato and numerous varieties of vegetables, fruits, and nuts.

1890s..Hugo de Vries conducts formal scientific research on the mechanisms of plant genetics.

1896–1940................................George Washington Carver makes significant contributions to agronomy, horticulture, and food technology.

1924 ....Clarence Birdseye fast-freezes
fish, taking food preservation to a
new level.

1928–1940................................Alexander Fleming discovers
penicillin and helps develop it into a
life-saving, mass-produced
pharmaceutical, thus ushering in the
age of antibiotics and profoundly
changing the practice of medicine.

1930s...Nikolai Vavilov studies living plans
to learn about the origins of
domesticated species.

1940s–1950s...............................Robert Braidwood employs
archaeological approaches to advance
the study of agricultural origins.

1940s–1970s ....Carbon dating and other direct
dating techniques are developed
and refined.

1953 ....James Watson and Francis Crick
publish their model for DNA
structure, giving impetus to the age
of molecular biology and ultimately
revolutionizing the fields of plant,
animal, and microbial genetics.

1964 ....The first clinical success of animal-
to-human xenotransplantation is
achieved when a chimpanzee kidney
is transplanted into a 23-year-old
woman, who survived for 9 months
after the operation.

c. 1966.......................................Norman Borlaug kicks off the green
revolution, greatly expanding the
world's food supply.

1967 ....Christiaan Barnard carries out the
first successful heart transplant.

1970–1979..................................	Bluefin tuna are raised from eggs in confinement and begin to spawn in confinement, providing a promising source of feedstock for the burgeoning fish-farming industry.
1974	U.S. Secretary of Agriculture Earl Butts tells American farmers to "get big or get out," thus moving one of the world's largest food-producing nations toward a vertically integrated, industrialized farming model.
1990	Human serum albumin is produced by a transgenic plant.
1995	Transgenic pigs, capable of producing human regulatory proteins, are constructed.
1996	Dolly the sheep is the first mammal to be successfully cloned.
c. 1998......................................	The ability to rapidly sequence DNA makes it possible to elucidate the human genome and the genomes of the plants, animals, and microbes of greatest interest to humans.
2000	Genetically engineered foods are common in the diet of Americans but remain controversial in much of the world.
2001	Pigs engineered to knock out certain genes whose products elicit immune reactions from human beings are cloned.
2009	The U.S. Food and Drug Administration approves the first drug produced by a pharm animal: a human protein expressed in the milk of a specially engineered transgenic goat.

Glossary

agronomy: A branch of agricultural science dealing with soils and management of field crop production.

antibody: A part of the mammalian immune system, antibodies are proteins produced by specialized cells that react with, bind to, destroy, or inactivate "foreign" substances known as antigens.

antigen: Any molecule (usually a protein or large carbohydrate) that can be specifically identified as "foreign" by an immune system. Once such recognition takes place, the immune system uses a variety of approaches to eliminate, degrade, or inactivate the antigen.

antithrombin: A protein found in blood that helps control blood clotting. Human antithrombin was produced and isolated from transgenic goats in 2009.

artificial insemination: The use of mechanical, nonnatural methods to place semen in the uterus or oviduct. This method can be used to permit a small number of genetically selected individuals to be sperm donors in a vast number of matings.

asynchronous germination: The tendency of some plants to produce seeds that are heterogeneous with regard to dormancy or readiness for germination. As a result, some seeds will germinate in the first growing season, but others will remain dormant until subsequent growing seasons. This increases the chance of having some seeds germinate when conditions are favorable for further growth.

aurochs (*Bos primigenius*): A type of wild cattle, now extinct, that ranged North Africa, Asia, and Europe. It was a very large animal, with the males standing over 6 feet at the shoulder and weighing well over 1 ton. They are thought to be the progenitors of modern cattle breeds.

autocatalytic: A reaction or set of conditions that will continue to completion without addition of other materials or changes in the environment.

biotic potential: The reproductive capacity of a species; that is, the maximum number of offspring that could be produced if there were no limiting factors in the environment.

BP: Before present.

breed: A group of animals presumed to be related by descent and exhibiting characteristic inheritable traits.

carbon dating: A way of assigning an age to an organic specimen by calculating the ratio of radioactive carbon 14 to the stable isotope carbon 12. Knowing the half-life of carbon 14 then permits determination of the age of the object.

carrying capacity: The maximum size of the population of an organism that an environment can support and sustain.

chromosomes: Structures in the nucleus of eukaryotic cells made of DNA and protein. They are the physical location of the genes and are visible under a microscope during mitosis and meiosis.

clone: An individual or group of organisms descended from a single individual through asexual reproduction. A clone should be genetically identical to the creature that gave rise to its nuclear DNA.

coevolution: The evolution of 2 or more species due to their interactions with each other over extended periods of time.

Columbian exchange: A term developed by Alfred W. Crosby Jr. to describe the ongoing passage of plants, animals, microbes, and people in both directions between the Old World and the New World, which began with the voyages of Christopher Columbus.

concentrated animal feeding operation (CAFO): An operation in which animals are concentrated together for efficiency in feeding and handling. These operations can often contain as many or more animals than the human population of a major city.

cultivar: A plant that has been maintained for multiple generations under cultivation or management.

diploid: A complete set of chromosome pairs in the nucleus.

environmental pressure: The combination of forces in the environment inclined to limit population size, such as predation, lack of resources, and parasitism.

eukaryotic: Plants, animals, fungi, and protists that are composed of cells that contain a membrane-bound nucleus, mitochondria, and other membrane-bound subcellular structures.

feral animal: An animal that has escaped from domestication and returned to the wild.

Fertile Crescent: A region in Southwest Asia bounded by the eastern Mediterranean, the Zagros Mountains, and the Negev Desert. It encompasses grasslands and open woodlands and was the site of much of the earliest agricultural activity, including the domestication of a number of important animals and plants.

flight response: The reaction of an animal to sensed predation risk or other perceived danger stimuli.

genetic engineering: The use of recombinant DNA technology to manipulate genes in ways to produce organisms that usually could not be produced by conventional genetic approaches. For example, genes are often moved from one species to another to produce transgenics.

genetic production platform: This is a phrase used to describe the entire synthesis and delivery system for a product made by molecular farming. For example, it is possible to speak of a molecule being made on either a plant or an animal production platform.

genotype: The genetic makeup or constitution of an individual.

green revolution: A set of advances in agronomy and plant genetics often associated with the work of Norman Borlaug. It resulted in vastly improved systems of grain production.

haploid: A nucleus containing just one member of each chromosome pair.

hexaploid: A nucleus containing 3 sets of each pair of chromosomes.

homeokinesis: The establishment of stability brought about by dynamic processes.

hominid: The group of all upright-walking, mammalian primates including anatomically modern humans and extinct related types.

Homo sapiens sapiens: The scientific name for anatomically modern humans, who made their appearance in sub-Saharan Africa approximately 200,000 years ago.

horticulturists: Defined here as members of an agricultural community that is committed to growing plants as the primary way of producing food.

hybridize: In genetics this term means to combine different strains or organisms to produce a type that contains genetic information from both donors.

immunosuppression: In organ transplant or xenotransplantation, the intentional suppression of the recipient immune system to minimize the threat of rejection of the transplanted tissue.

industrial strain: A group of animals selected as a subset of a standard breed. The selections are scientifically conducted to produce animals that are exquisitely suited to a specific sort of production system. The individuals are not registered in a public herd or flock book, because the genetic package that these animals constitute is owned by the people that produced it.

keystone species: A species that has a disproportionately impact on its environment, beyond its numbers or its mass. Removal of a keystone species generally results in collapse of the environment.

knock-out approach: This is an informal term used by geneticists when discussing approaches that will eliminate a gene or keep a gene from being expressed. Thus the gene is said to be knocked out.

landrace: A geographically isolated group of animals in which the natural conditions and the aims and goals of the herdsman provide selective pressures resulting in a distinct, recognizable type. The formation of a landrace is often the first step toward the development of a standard breed.

leghemoglobin: An oxygen-carrying protein produced by certain leguminous plants in response to infection of their roots by nitrogen-fixing bacteria. This protein removes oxygen from the area of infection producing the anaerobic conditions necessary for symbiotic nitrogen fixation.

mass spectrometer: A scientific instrument used to measure the mass of atoms. It is capable of separating and quantifying different isotopes of the same element. It is also an essential tool in determining the age of a carbon-containing object by carbon dating.

meiosis: The process that results in the formation of gametes, or sex cells, in eukaryotes. It consists of 2 successive nuclear divisions in which the 2N nucleus of the parent cell gives rise to four 1N gametes.

Mesolithic: A transitional archaeological period in which stone tools of a type more sophisticated and finer than those of the Paleolithic were produced.

midden: A refuse heap or dumping place. Archaeologists often find ancient middens to be veritable treasure troves of objects that shed light on the culture that produced them.

mitochondrial genetics: Hereditary studies conducted on the maternally inherited DNA of the mitochondria. This approach can be very useful in determining relatedness of members of the same species or genus.

mitosis: Division of the eukaryotic nucleus resulting in 2 daughter nuclei with the same number of chromosomes as the parent nucleus.

molecular farming: The use of transgenic plants to produce molecules of medical, pharmacological, or commercial importance.

mouflon: A kind of wild sheep, the male of which has large curving horns. They were once common in the western Mediterranean region but are now restricted in the wild to mountaintop ranges on Corsica and Sardinia. They are thought to be the wild progenitors of modern domestic sheep.

mutualism (mutualistic symbiosis): A term used by biologists to describe 2 species living together in such a way that benefit is derived by both species.

natural selection: A natural process whereby the members of a population with the genetic makeup best suited to the environment enjoy the greatest reproductive success, resulting in continual genetic adjustment of the population to prevailing conditions.

negative feedback: A kind of regulatory mechanism, generally with a set point that tends to move a system in the opposite direction of a perturbation. Negative feedback is essential in maintaining homeostasis.

Neolithic: The last of the archaeological periods known as the Stone Age. The Neolithic is characterized by polished stone tools. Toward the end of the Neolithic period, human beings first began cultivating and herding animals and later domesticated plants and animals.

Neolithic Revolution: The transition from hunting and gathering as a way of life to active food production through domestication of plants and animals and dependence on agriculture to produce the bulk of human nutrients.

nitrogen fixation: The reduction of atmospheric nitrogen (molecular nitrogen) to the level of ammonia. This process can be conducted in nature only by certain prokaryotic organisms, some of which carry out the process in a symbiotic relationship with leguminous plants.

nitrogenase: An enzyme produced by prokaryotic organisms capable of reducing molecular nitrogen to the level that it can be incorporated into organic material.

Paleolithic: An archaeological period known for the production of crude stone tools. This period dates back to before the appearance of anatomically modern humans and spans most of the early history of that species.

pangenesis: A theory of heredity supported by Charles Darwin in which it was thought that elements of heredity called gemules circulated in the blood, coalesced in the gonads, and were ultimately concentrated in the reproductive cells. This theory received little experimental support and was completely supplanted by the Mendelian theory of inheritance.

parasitism: A symbiotic relationship in which one partner, the parasite, benefits and the other partner, the host, is damaged by the interaction.

pastoralists: Subsistence agriculturists that make their living primarily by tending flocks or herds of large animals.

pharm animal: A transgenic domesticated animal constructed for the purpose of producing useful pharmaceutical products in its milk, blood, or tissues.

phenotype: The anatomical, physiological, or behavioral expressions of an individual's genes.

plasmid: Small, circular DNA molecule found in some bacteria. Plasmids carry genes not found in the main bacterial DNA. Molecular biologists and genetic engineers frequently employ these structures in techniques involving the replication, manipulation, and transfer of genes.

positive feedback: This is a type of response to a stimulus or perturbation that moves the system in the same direction as the perturbation. Rather than leading to a stable situation as negative feedback often does, positive feedback causes an accelerating or cascading movement in one direction until the system changes.

prokaryotic: The kind of cell that defines the members of the kingdoms Monera and Archaea. These cells do not contain true nuclei or membrane-bound subcellular organelles, but they do sometimes have internal membrane systems.

protodog: A type of wolf, the existence of which is inferred by zoologists interested in the formation of domestic dogs. It is thought that this was a naturally occurring wolf variant that may have been smaller, less aggressive, and more tolerant of the presence of humans than other wolves.

quaternary care hospital: The highest level designation for a health-care facility based on the level of sophistication of subspecialty care available. Such hospitals can routinely perform organ transplants and may engage in molecular and genetic medicine.

rachis: The main axis or spike of a grain by which individual spikelets are attached to the plant.

salinization: The deposition of salt. This can occur in soils that are irrigated if the irrigation water evaporates or if ground water brings up salts from the subsoil that are deposited when the water evaporates.

secondary metabolite: Compounds produced by an organism that are not directly involved in the growth, development, or reproduction of the organism.

standard breeds: Related groups of animals exhibiting characteristics that are described in a written breed standard. The animals are registered in some form of record book, and matings are restricted so as to permit breeding only among registered animals that conform to the breed standard.

synchronous germination: A tendency of some plants to have all their seeds germinate in the same growing season.

tarpan: A subspecies of wild horse, now extinct. Some zoologists consider the tarpan to be the progenitor of the modern horse.

teosinte: An annual grass that grows wild in Mexico and Guatemala and is known to be the wild progenitor of modern maize (corn).

tetraploid: Possessing 2 sets of each pair of chromosomes; in other words, having twice the diploid number or 4 times the monoploid number of chromosomes.

transgenic: A plant, animal, or microbe containing DNA and genes from another species. Such creatures are made possible by recombinant DNA technology, which takes advantage of the universal nature of the genetic code.

xenotransplantation (xenografting): The surgical joining or grafting of an organ or tissue from one species onto another.

zoonotic disease: A malady caused by infectious agents that can be passed from animals to humans or that is shared by animals and humans.

Biographical Notes

Appert, Nicolas (1749–1841): Appert is known as the Father of Canning because he invented a method for the long-term preservation of plant and animal material in glass jars using heat to kill off the microbes generally associated with food spoilage. The combination of heat and anaerobic conditions combined to effectively preserve a number of foods. Appert got his start in this business by entering a competition held by Napoleon Bonaparte for the preservation of foodstuffs that could be used to feed his army. After winning a prize of 12,000 francs for his method, Appert worked to perfect it. About 10 years later, he established the House of Appert—the world's first canning company.

Bakewell, Robert (1725–1795): Bakewell was a member of England's landed gentry. On his farm near Dishley he practiced systematic, if not scientific, breeding of livestock. He greatly improved the quality of Britain's sheep, horses, and cattle. In addition to making a number of very productive crosses, he practiced inbreeding to "fix" some of the traits that he favored. He knew the importance of getting others to practice the sort of record keeping and controlled breeding that he did, and as a result he was instrumental in developing breeding societies to preserve some of the strains that he developed.

Barnard, Christiaan (1922–2001): Barnard was a South African cardiothoracic surgeon. Following his medical training in South Africa, he studied and practiced for several years at the University of Minnesota, where he came in contact with some of the pioneers in organ-transplant surgery. After returning to South Africa, he built up a surgical team, which like several others around the world was poised to attempt a human-to-human heart transplant. In 1967, he and his team completed the first successful heart transplant, and though the patient lived only a little over 2 weeks before succumbing to pneumonia brought on by the necessary immunosuppressive regimen, Barnard and his colleagues had opened the door to what would become a successful, life-extending branch of surgery.

Beadle, George (1903–1989): Beadle was an American geneticist who received the Nobel Prize in Physiology and Medicine in 1958 for work that he did with his colleague, Edward Tatum, on gene expression in the bread mold *Neurospora crassa* in the early 1940s.

Throughout his career, Beadle had strong interests in agronomy and plant genetics. He had a markedly successful career as president of the University of Chicago. After he retired from university administration, he and his colleagues ultimately demonstrated that an inconspicuous plant, teosinte, was the evolutionary progenitor of *Zea maize*.

Birdseye, Clarence (1886–1956): Birdseye, a pioneer in the use of quick freezing for the preservation of fish, other seafood, meats, vegetables, and fruits, became aware of the potential of the method by spending time with the Inuit in Labrador. He appreciated that quick freezing resulted in the formation of smaller ice crystals than did the slower freezing methods being employed in the early years of the 20th century. The smaller crystals did less damage to the cellular structure of the material being frozen, reducing the impact on appearance, texture, and taste. Birdseye was instrumental in developing packaging and distribution methods that made frozen foods commonplace in the developed world of the 20th and 21st centuries.

Borlaug, Norman (b. 1914): In the middle years of the last century, Norman Borlaug, employing standard plant-breeding approaches, developed a number of high-yielding, disease-resistant strains of wheat. He and his colleagues were able to vastly improve the output of wheat farms in Mexico by introducing these strains and employing modern agricultural production techniques and educational programs to give Mexican farmers and scientists ongoing capacities in the area of wheat production. Similar results were then obtained in Pakistan and India. In each case, Borlaug made the people of these countries much more food secure, and he is credited with having saved multitudes of people from starvation. This work later came to be known as the green revolution; for his contributions, Borlaug was awarded the Nobel Peace Prize in 1970.

Braidwood, Robert (1907–2003): Educated as an architect, Braidwood was quickly drawn to archaeology and joined the University of Chicago's Oriental Institute. Equipped with skills in carbon dating artifacts, he made significant progress in elucidating the events that lead to early food production in the Middle East. He is often credited with developing the archaeological approach to questions relating to the origins of agriculture.

Burbank, Luther (1849–1926): Burbank was a widely heralded American botanist and horticulturist. He reached almost celebrity status during his lifetime for the remarkable number of new flower, fruit, vegetable, and nut varieties that he developed. Born on a New England farm, he received little formal education but was a gifted observer and became an essentially self-taught plant breeder. Among the many well-known cultivars that he developed are the freestone peach and the Burbank russet potato. The latter is the most widely cultivated potato in the world today and serves as the starting material for McDonald's French fries.

Carver, George Washington (1864–1943): Born as a slave near the end of the American Civil War, George Washington Carver might seem unlikely to emerge as one of the most original, creative, and broadly based plant scientists and agriculturists in the history of the world. He and his mother were "stolen" by Confederate Night Riders. He was reclaimed by Moses and Susan Carver after the war, who raised him as their own child, as his mother was never found again and the identity of his father was uncertain. The young Carver faced many racial and social barriers to his pursuit of a formal education. He eventually graduated from Simpson College in Iowa, which offered no science courses, Carver's principal interest, at that time. After graduation with a degree in Piano and Art, he entered what today is Iowa State University, where he received an M.S. in Bacterial Botany. Shortly thereafter, he joined the university's faculty, becoming its first black faculty member. He was persuaded by Booker T. Washington to join the faculty of the Tuskegee Institute as Director of Agriculture. Carver spent the rest of his life at Tuskegee, where he made significant contributions to soil science, teaching farmers the benefits of alternating soil-enriching crops with king cotton, which was notorious for soil depletion. He did extensive research in plant and food chemistry, fields in which he held numerous U.S. patents. It is a wonderful irony that a son of slaves is the person most widely credited with assisting the southern United States to convert from a single-crop economic system dependent on slaves and notorious for soil degradation and depletion to a verdant multicrop system with much greater sustainability and overall productivity.

Clement VIII (pope; 1536–1605): Probably best known for his suppression and execution of the philosopher Giordano Bruno, Clement lived in a time when the church was confronting the emergence of Protestantism. The Jubilee of 1600 was celebrated during his papacy, and during his time in St. Peter's, he did much to shore up the holding of the Papal States. He is included here because of a claim that he make coffee a drink fit for good Christians by baptizing it. It is not clear that he ever actually baptized the drink, but he did apparently state that baptism would be appropriate to spite the devil for giving such a wonderful drink to the Muslims.

Columbus, Christopher (1451–1505): Christopher Columbus was a Genoese seafarer, navigator, and adventurer. Though controversy continues concerning who "discovered" America, there can be no doubt that it was the voyages of Columbus in 1492 and 1493 that established ongoing interaction between the New World and Europe. Though born in what today is Italy, Columbus made his history-altering voyages and discoveries under the flag of Spain, and it was primarily through Spain that the first exchanges of plants and animals between the New World and the Old World took place.

Darwin, Charles (1809–1882): Charles Darwin was the grandson of Erasmus Darwin and the cousin of Francis Galton. One of the middle children in a large family, the young Darwin had difficulties finding a profession that would satisfy his father. He tried both medicine and the clergy before embarking on his famous multiyear voyage as naturalist on HMS *Beagle*. In the years following his return, he married well, raised a family, and began to establish himself as the preeminent naturalist of his day. However, it was his work on descent with modification and the origin of species that earned him recognition as one of the greatest and most influential thinkers in modern history. He studied domestication in animals and plants and wrote extensively on the subject. In fact, it was his observations on domesticates and the impact of selective breeding that helped him develop his theory of natural selection.

Darwin, Erasmus (1731–1802): The grandfather of Charles Darwin and Francis Galton, Erasmus Darwin was a genuine polymath. One of the leading intellectuals of his time, he was a philosopher, physician, naturalist, and poet. It should be noted that as a naturalist, he actually formulated a theory of evolution, but unlike his grandson Charles, he could provide no plausible mechanism for the process.

Nonetheless, in his well-known and oft-quoted poem *The Temple of Nature*, he presages the discovery of the microbial world and some of the current thinking on prebiotic evolution, suggesting that life began with microscopic organisms arising from inorganic material in the primordial oceans.

de Vries, Hugo (1848–1935): Early in his career, de Vries became fascinated with the evolutionary theory of Charles Darwin; despite the skepticism of his faculty mentors, de Vries continued his interest as he began work on agricultural crops. Influenced by Darwin's thinking, de Vries began the study of pangenesis. He focused on the particles, or gemmules, that were supposed to be controlling heredity. He called them pangenes, which was later shortened to "genes"; as a result, de Vries is credited with coining that term. Toward the end of the 19th century, de Vries became familiar with the earlier work of Mendel, which had been all but forgotten for nearly 40 years. He independently verified Mendel's work and worked to synthesize it into Darwin's evolutionary theory. During his lifetime, de Vries was known for constructing interesting varieties of the evening primrose. He ultimately developed his own variant on evolutionary theory, known as the mutation theory. It did not deal with what is now called genetic mutation but did argue within evolutionary theory that Darwinian gradualism may not be correct.

Fleming, Alexander (1881–1955): Fleming was born in Scotland but pursued his career as a bacteriologist and physician in England. He served with distinction in the British Army Medical Corps in World War I and, following the war, began research on vaccine therapy and influenza. It was during those studies that he made the discovery for which he is best known. Countless bacteriologists before him had been frustrated by fungal contamination of their bacterial cultures. Fleming's serendipitous observation that a mold contaminant on one of his plates was surrounded by a clear, bacteria-free zone suggested that the mold was producing some form of antibacterial agent. Fleming isolated this substance and named it penicillin. Though he shared the Nobel Prize with 2 other scientists whose work was instrumental in the development and production of penicillin as a practical antimicrobial drug, Fleming is generally thought of as the father of the antibiotic age in medicine.

Galton, Francis (1822–1911): Francis Galton was the grandson of Erasmus Darwin and the cousin of Charles Darwin. There can be little doubt that Galton was a true genius. His interests were as wide ranging as those of his grandfather, and his capacities for deep and critical thought were on a par with those of his illustrious cousin. Galton made significant contributions to applied mathematics and statistics. He used his expertise in this field in the study of human characteristics such as intelligence. He was an early worker in the field of eugenics and is credited with coining that term. Galton and Charles Darwin had a continuing correspondence concerning the theory of pangenesis, which Darwin was proposing as the genetic mechanism behind his theory of natural selection. Galton undertook studies on pangenesis and essentially disproved the concept. In the progress of that work, he came close to making the same discoveries as Mendel, but he tended to focus on polygenic rather than discrete traits, thus making his observations substantially more difficult to interpret than those of Mendel. He also undertook studies on the process of domestication and promulgated several characteristics that an animal should possess if it is to become a successful domesticate.

George III (king; 1738–1820): George III was king of England during the rebellion in the American colonies, and his handling of the affairs of state at that time caused him to be remembered as the monarch who lost the Americas. By most accounts, he was ill prepared for the tasks of governing and trusted much of his responsibility for governing to a series of advisors. He was not well loved by his subjects, who often referred to him as Farmer George in reference to his crude, rustic speech and lack of refinement. However, that title may have been apt, since this rather poor monarch was apparently a very engaged and successful farmer. He was interested in the agricultural technology of the day and paid a great deal of attention to the improvement of livestock. It has even been claimed that he turned a profit by grazing and cropping the lawns around Windsor. He suffered from an inherited disease called porphyria, which very likely was responsible for his repeated bouts of madness and delirium.

Jefferson, Thomas (1743–1826): A man of remarkable intellectual gifts, Thomas Jefferson remains one of the United States' most enigmatic figures. As principal author of the Declaration of Independence, third president of the United States, and founder of the University of Virginia, this planter, statesman, philosopher, and architect remains a towering figure in American history. He commissioned the Lewis and Clark expedition that opened much of the western United States to further expansion. As a member of the planter class, Jefferson became committed to an agricultural system based on large farms on which a cash crop (cotton) was essentially grown as a monoculture. Since cotton is notorious for depleting the soil, there were only 2 courses such a planter could follow in order to stay in business: Expend the requisite time, treasure, and labor to restore the soil; or move on and find other land to plant. Jefferson was known to say that it was easier to get a new acre than manure an old one. The end result of this form of land use was to take more land with an army of soldiers, work it with an army of slaves, and leave the depleted soil behind.

Little, Charles Cook (1881–1971): As a young boy, Charles Little kept mice as a hobby. Thus, he was very familiar with the care and maintenance of these animals when he entered Harvard University and began to study the Mendelian genetics of their coat color. It was apparent to Little and others that it was essential to have laboratory strains that would breed true; that is, that each of their quantifiable or observable genetic traits would be faithfully reproduced upon mating. The method used to fix a trait or ensure that the organism is homozygous for it is to carry out extensive inbreeding. Little was successful in producing several strains that essentially bred true for all the characteristics and traits of interest, but the genetic strain of such extensive inbreeding greatly weakened these strains, making them less-than-ideal laboratory specimens. Sometime around 1914, Little started with 2 promising laboratory mice and inbred them through at least 20 generations. The resulting strain, dubbed "black 6," had some inherited weakness but reproduced vigorously and was reasonably easy to maintain. Over time, it became the most widely used inbred strain of mouse for the study of mammalian genetics. In 2002, the black 6 was the first nonhuman to have its genome sequenced.

Mendel, Gregor (1822–1884): Working alone in the garden of an Augustinian monastery in what is now the Czech Republic, the young Mendel conducted experiments on a variety of pea plants that laid the groundwork for scientific genetics and established the particulate nature of the hereditary determinants later called genes. Mendel first presented his findings in 1865, but because of his isolation from the mainstream of scientific thought and the obscurity of the monastery in which he lived, this seminal work was essentially lost until rediscovered in the early 20th century by Hugo de Vries and others. Mendel's discoveries bolstered the theory of evolution proposed by Charles Darwin and supplied a plausible genetic mechanism to support natural selection.

Pfister, Lester (1897–1970): A man with little formal education, Lester Pfister demonstrated the sort of perseverance and drive that so characterized successful business leaders in the lean years preceding World War II. From childhood, Pfister was driven to develop and grow superior strains of corn. On his farm near El Paso, Illinois, he experimented with production of hybrid corn seed. At that time, it was essential to control self-pollination by covering the male and female reproductive structures with paper bags. Pfister could often be seen tying such bags to his corn plants, earning him the nickname Crazy Lester. He was, however, crazy like a fox: In the face of considerable financial difficulty, he was able to convince local bankers to back his seed corn enterprise. In the following decades, he was able to build his company into the largest and one of the most successful hybrid seed corn companies in the world. He also had a creative flair when it came to farm machinery, developing improved corn pickers, detasseling machines, and improved spraying machinery for insect control.

Vavilov, Nikolai Ivanovitch (1887–1943): Vavilov was one of the leading plant geneticists of his day. He is credited with developing what is known as the biological approach to understanding the centers of origin of agricultural practice and domestication of plants. Vavilov was called upon to help modernize Soviet agriculture and increase food production through application of scientific approaches. He succeeded in establishing more than 400 research institutes throughout the Soviet Union. However, he fell into political disfavor when he was opposed by a politically connected hack with bizarre ideas about science. Vavilov was arrested in front of his students and colleagues in one of his research plots and died in custody in 1943, a victim of intrusion of politics and dogma into science.

Washington, George (1732–1799): Washington was a member of the planter class in Virginia. He gained military experience fighting in the French and Indian War. He later served as the commander of the Continental Army during the Revolutionary War and became the first president of the United States. Washington was a very careful, frugal, and progressive farmer. He kept excellent records, paid close attention to the management of Mount Vernon, and studied animal husbandry. He constructed a number of innovative agricultural structures, including a 16-sided treading barn. He may have been America's first serious composter and expended care and effort in improving his soil. He felt that the future of America was dependent upon the adoption of progressive agricultural practices, and to that end, he encouraged the development of agricultural societies. The oldest of these was the Philadelphia Society for Promoting Agriculture, founded in 1785. Washington was the fist honorary member of that society, and I was privileged to serve a term as president of that organization, which is still working for the cause of agricultural progress.

Bibliography

Because of the interdisciplinary nature of this course and the substantial period of time that it covers, there is no single text available that covers all subjects treated in the lectures. The work by Bruce D. Smith comes as close as any in providing background for the first half of the course. Unfortunately, there is no single source dealing with the range of subjects covered in the second portion. Consequently, I have provided a number of works that contain useful information and background on most of the subjects covered. I have also provided a few sentences to describe the content and coverage of each in an effort to assist students in finding additional material on any of the subjects in which they develop particular interest. All of the books listed can be obtained from a collegiate library, through interlibrary loan, or from online providers.

Albala, Ken. *Beans—A History*. Oxford: Berg, 2007. From lentils to soybeans, this book traces the domestication, cultivation, and processing of the "poor man's meat" and gives a rich dollop of the social significance of these pod-born domesticates.

Anthony, David W. *The Horse, the Wheel and Language—How Bronze-Age Riders from the Eurasian Steppes Shaped the Modern World*. Princeton, NJ: Princeton University Press, 2007. This book uses anthropology, archaeology, and linguistics to elucidate the role played by domesticated horses and wheeled vehicles in dispersing the first speakers of Proto-Indo-European.

Balter, Michael. "Seeking Agriculture's Ancient Roots." *Science* 316 (2007): 1830–1835. This review article does a fine job of summarizing some of the more recent advances in the study of the origins of agriculture.

Bellwood, Peter. *First Farmers—The Origins of Agricultural Societies*. Oxford: Blackwell, 2005. This is a scholarly, up-to-date presentation of the origins and spread of agriculture. It deals with plant and animal domestication; the dispersal of farming culture; and attempts to correlate archaeology, linguistics, and genetics in these studies.

Betsch, David F. "Pharmaceutical Production from Transgenic Animals." *North Central Regional Extension Publication* 552 (1995). This is a useful review of the methods used to make transgenic animals for the production of pharmaceuticals.

Bosland, Paul W. "Capsicums: Innovative Uses of an Ancient Crop." In *Progress in New Crops*, edited by J. Janic, 479–487. Arlington, VA: ASHS Press, 1996. This article provides a good background on the history of cultivation, the breadth of species, and the interesting products of these peppers.

Bovine HapMap Consortium. "Genome-Wide Survey of SNP Variation Uncovers the Genetic Structure of Cattle Breeds." *Science* 324 (2009): 528–532. This genomic study of cattle breeds shows a distinct narrowing of the gene pool of cattle due to domestication when compared to the very broad genetic range of the ancestors of modern cattle breeds.

Budiansky, Stephen. *The Covenant of the Wild—Why Animals Chose Domestication*. Leesburg, VA: Terrapin Press at Black Sheep Farm, 1995. This small book makes a compelling case for the "partnership" developed between humans and their domesticated animals and the mutual dependency that has developed over the past 10 millennia.

Carlson, Laurie Winn. *Cattle—An Informal Social History*. Chicago: Ivan R. Dee, 2001. This informal treatment of the domestication of cattle and the development of the cattle culture deals with subjects ranging from initial domestication to free-speech issues related to meat consumption.

Chessa, Bernardo, Filipe Pereira, Frederick Arnaud, Antonio Amorim, Félix Goyache, Ingrid Mainland, Rowland R. Kao, et al. "Revealing the History of Sheep Domestication Using Retrovirus Integrations." *Science* 324 (2009): 532–536. This article, employing a genetic approach, provides a model for the initial domestication and spread of "primitive" and modern sheep breeds.

Chrispeels, Maarten J., and David Sadava. *Plants, Food, and People*. San Francisco: W. H. Freeman and Company, 1977. This is an older book, but it can still be found in many college libraries. It presents a very well-organized treatment of early plant domestication, basic agricultural practice, plant breeding, and implications for human nutrition. It is an excellent general reference.

Clutton-Brock, Juliet. *Domesticated Animals from Early Times*. Austin: University of Texas Press, 1981.

Cochran, Gregory, and Henry Harpending. *The 10,000 Year Explosion—How Civilization Accelerated Human Evolution*. New York: Basic Books, 2009. This book takes a bold approach to previously taboo subjects, dealing with the genetic differences among the world's peoples, which the authors claim have accelerated as a result of the rise of civilization.

Creasy, Rosalind. *The Edible Heirloom Garden*. Boston: Periplus Editions, 1999. Richly illustrated with color photographs, this volume provides pictures of and recipes employing a wide array of heirloom plants and vegetables.

Crosby, Alfred W., Jr. *The Columbian Exchange—Biological and Cultural Consequences of 1492*. Westport, CT: Praeger, 2003. This is the definitive book dealing with the ongoing exchange of plants, animals, people, and disease between the New World and the Old World.

Curry, Andrew. "The World's First Temple?" *Smithsonian*, November 2008, 54. This article describes the archaeological investigation of Gobekli Tepe, a site in Turkey that may hold some important clues to the earliest conversions to agricultural practices by hunting-gathering peoples.

Darwin, Charles. *The Variation of Animals and Plants under Domestication*. Vol. 1. London: Johns Hopkins Press, 1868. This classic work has been issued in several editions and has been in print since it was first published. It followed *On the Origin of Species* and was an attempt by Darwin to demonstrate the reality of evolution to anyone who cared to look closely at common domesticated animals.

Diamond, Jared. *Guns, Germs, and Steel: The Fates of Human Societies*. New York: W. W. Norton, 1997. Though somewhat controversial in its central premise, this book provides an excellent description of what is known about the transition from hunting and gathering to food production as well as the long-lasting implications of that fundamental conversion in our way of obtaining necessary nourishment.

Dillehay, T. D., J. Rossen, T. C. Andres, and D. E. Williams. "Preceramic Adoption of Peanut, Squash, and Cotton in Northern Peru." *Science* 316 (2007): 1890–1893. This article provides good background on the early development of agriculture and horticultural communities in a part of the New World.

Dohner, Janet Vorwald. *The Encyclopedia of Historic and Endangered Livestock and Poultry Breeds.* New Haven, CT: Yale University Press, 2001. This is a well-illustrated and carefully researched volume containing detailed information on the domestication and history of a large number of breeds of livestock and poultry.

Dubcovsky, Jorge, and Jan Dvorak. "Genome Plasticity a Key Factor in the Success of Polyploid Wheat under Domestication." *Science* 316 (2007): 1862–1866. This is a genomic study of the spread and adaptability of domesticated wheat; it contains good background information on the genomics of initial domestication events.

Elsik, C. G., R. L. Tellam, and K. C. Worley. "The Genome Sequence of Taurine Cattle: A Window to Ruminant Biology and Evolution." *Science* 324 (2009): 522–528. This article relies on the genome sequence of cattle to explore mammalian evolution and the separation of cattle from other ruminants.

Fogel, Robert William. *The Escape from Hunger and Premature Death, 1700–2100—Europe, America, and the Third World.* Cambridge: Cambridge University Press, 2004. This small book deals insightfully with the connections between agricultural production, economic and social inequality, and basic nutrition. It addresses the 18th century to the present and projects into the future.

Fusonie, Alan, and Donna Jean Fusonie. *George Washington— Pioneer Farmer.* Mount Vernon, VA: Mount Vernon Ladies Association, 1998. This volume details George Washington's commitment to careful stewardship of the land and to progressive and inventive approaches to plant and animal agriculture.

Hancock, J. F. *Plant Evolution and the Origin of Crop Species.* Cambridge, MA: CABI, 2004. This book combines discussions of plant evolution and the origin of domesticated crop plants. It deals with the origins of grains, garden vegetables, and fruits.

Harper, Charles L., and Bryan Le Beau. *Food, Society, and Environment.* Upper Saddle River, NJ: Pearson Education, 2003. This is a historical review of food production and consumption from our early hunter-gatherer ancestors to present day America. It treats these subjects with a view toward economics and social justice.

Hemmer, Helmut. *Domestication—The Decline of Environmental Appreciation.* Cambridge: Cambridge University Press, 1990. This book emphasizes the critical role animal domestication played in the development of human civilization. This work contains interesting discussion on the behavior of domesticates, semidomesticates, and feral animals.

Hesser, Leon. *The Man Who Fed the World—Nobel Peace Prize Laureate Norman Borlaug and His Battle to End World Hunger.* Dallas, TX: Durban House, 2006. This is a biography of Norman Borlaug, who is often credited with launching the green revolution. It provides a useful history of the development of a number of international plant-breeding and agronomic organizations and their role in the development of a truly global food-production system.

Hillel, Daniel. *Out of the Earth—Civilization and the Life of the Soil.* Berkeley: University of California Press, 1991. The author deals with ancient and prehistoric land-use issues and the impact that the agricultural way of life has on soil productivity.

Jones, M. K., and X. Liu. "Origins of Agriculture in East Asia." *Science* 324 (2009): 730–731. This article describes cereal grain domestication in East Asia and stresses that the conversion to the use of domesticated varieties was gradual and may have been almost imperceptible to those doing the cultivation of the crops.

Kennedy, Roger G. *Mr. Jefferson's Lost Cause—Land, Farmers, Slavery and the Louisiana Purchase.* Oxford: Oxford University Press, 2003. This book provides marvelous examples of the profound impact on the history of human civilization brought about by decisions on land use and which domesticates to cultivate.

Knutson, Ronald D., J. B. Penn, and Barry L. Flinchbaugh. *Agriculture and Food Policy.* 5th ed. Upper Saddle River, NJ: Pearson/Prentice Hall, 2004. This book provides an excellent exploration of the interplay of food-production decisions, economics, and the fates of nations and people in the modern world.

Koeppel, Dan. *Banana—The Fate of the Fruit That Changed the World.* New York: Hudson Street Press, 2008. The author interweaves biology, history, economics, and politics as he tells the fascinating story of the development of a powerful international industry built around the cultivation and marketing of a single domesticated plant.

Laszlo, Pierre. *Citrus—A History*. Chicago: University of Chicago Press, 2007. This volume covers the domestication, cultivation, and spread of citrus fruits from their points of origin to the precious citrus groves found in warm regions throughout the world. There is also interesting material on the cultural and religious aspects of human cultivation of these "exotic" plants.

Levetin, Estelle, and Karen McMahon. *Plants and Society*. 2nd ed. Boston: WCB/McGraw-Hill, 1999. This book is an excellent source of information on food, beverage, spice, and fiber plants. It deals with their domestication, spread, cultivation, and cultural significance.

Logan, William Bryant. *Oak—The Frame of Civilization*. New York: W. W. Norton, 2005. Though it deals with only a single tree species, this book provides interesting information on the role played by woody trees in the development of human civilization.

Ludwig, A., M. Pruvost, M. Reissman, N. Benecke, G. A. Brockman, P. Castanos, M. Cieslak, et al. "Coat Color Variation at the Beginning of Horse Domestication." *Science* 314 (2009): 485. This article is a genetic treatment of the role played by artificial selection in the domestication of the horse.

Madigan, M. T., J. M. Martinko, and J. Parker. *Brock Biology of Microorganisms*. 10th ed. Upper Saddle River, NJ: Pearson Education, 2002. This is a modern and up-to-date textbook of general microbiology that in addition to supporting the lecture on domesticated microorganisms also serves as a good source on genetic engineering and the formation of transgenic organisms.

Maisels, Charles Keith. *The Emergence of Civilization—From Hunting and Gathering to Agriculture, Cities, and the State in the Near East*. London: Routledge, 1990. This is an in-depth scholarly treatment of the domestication of plants and animals and the development and spread of agriculture in the Near East.

Michler, Robert E. "Xenotransplantation: Risks, Clinical Potential, and Future Prospects." *Emerging Infectious Diseases* 2, no. 1 (1996), http://www.cdc.gov/ncidod/eid/vol2no1/michler.htm. This is a well-referenced article covering the history, risks, and potential of xenotransplantation up to 1996.

Muehlbauer, F. J. "Food and Grain Legumes." In *New Crops*, edited by J. Janic and J. E. Simon, 256. New York: Wiley, 1993. This article deals briefly with the history of domestication of the chickpea, grasspea, fava bean, and lentil in the Fertile Crescent. It also describes modern cultivation of these important plants.

Nicholl, Desmond S. T. *An Introduction to Genetic Engineering.* 2nd ed. Cambridge: Cambridge University Press, 2002. This book provides a good basic discussion of the formation of transgenic plants and animals and their use in medicine, agriculture, and industry.

Normile, Dennis. "Persevering Researchers Make a Splash with Farm-Bred Tuna." *Science* 324 (2009): 1260–1261. This review of Japanese efforts to breed and raise bluefin tuna in captivity provides good background to the subject of farming the waters.

Pollack, Andrew. "FDA Approves Drug from Gene-Altered Goats." *The New York Times*, February 6, 2009. This article reports on the approval by the FDA of antithrombin made by transgenic goats and obtained in their milk. It provides a brief, general description of how this technique works.

Reed, Clarence A., and John Davidson. *The Improved Nut Trees of North America.* New York: Devlin-Adair, 1954.

Roberts, R. M., E. W. Smith, F. W. Bazer, J. Cibelli, G. E. Seidel Jr., D. E. Bauman, L. P. Reynolds, and J. J. Ireland. "Farm Animal Research in Crisis." *Science* 324 (2009): 468–469. This review article summarizes the use of some common farm animals for research in medicine and physiology.

Sharrer, Terry. "The First Black 6: C57BL/6J." *The Scientist*, January 2007, 84.

Smith, Bruce D. *The Emergence of Agriculture.* New York: Scientific American Library, 1995. This book comes as close to a standard text for the first half of this course as any other in the bibliography. It brings together information from a wide range of fields and disciplines to give a readable account of the emergence of agriculture around the globe.

Sponenberg, D. Philip, and Donald E. Bixby. *Managing Breeds for a Secure Future—Strategies for Breeders and Breed Associations.* Pittsboro, NC: American Livestock Breeds Conservancy, 2007. Although this is essentially an instruction book for active conservation breeders, it contains excellent discussions of what is implied and conveyed by the terms "breed," "landrace," and "feral animal." It is a useful source for the provenance and current status of a number of livestock breeds that originated elsewhere but played important roles in the development of the United States.

Surowiecki, James. "The Perils of Efficiency." *The New Yorker,* November 24, 2008, 46.

Sweeney, Del. *Agriculture in the Middle Ages: Technology, Practice, and Representation.* Philadelphia: University of Pennsylvania Press, 1995.

"Troubled Waters." *The Economist,* January 3, 2009, 3–18.

Wang, J., T. Gao, and S. Knapp. "Ancient Chinese Literature Reveals Pathways of Eggplant Domestication." *Annals of Botany* 102, no. 6 (2008): 891–897. This is a good example of how early plant domestications can be studied using the ancient literature of some cultures.

Wilson, Bee. "The Last Bite: Is the World's Food System Collapsing?" *The New Yorker,* May 19, 2008, 76–80.

Notes

Notes